# More CHRISTMAS ORNAMENTS TO CROCHET

## 36 NEW DESIGNS TO CELEBRATE a HANDMADE HOLIDAY

T0273868

Cedar Lane Press, PO Box 5424, Lancaster, PA 17606-5424

Paperback ISBN: 978-1-958212-02-8

ePub ISBN: 978-1-958212-03-5

Library of Congress Control Number available on request

Printed in the United States of America

10 9 8 7 6 5 4 3 2 1

Note: The following list contains names used in *More Christmas Ornaments to Crochet* that may be registered with the United States Copyright Office:

6060; American Felt & Craft; Beadsmith; Beadalon; Bead Landing; Cascade Heritage; Clover; Delta Sobo; Etsy; Glass Eyes Online; Fiskars; Hakko; Hobbs Bonded Fibers; Martha Stewart Crafts; Nature's Garden; Plaid; Sculpey; Sulky; "The 12 Days of Christmas"; *The Nutcracker*; Tulip

The information in this book is given in good faith; however, no warranty is given, nor are results guaranteed. Woodworking is inherently dangerous. Your safety is your responsibility. Neither Cedar Lane Press nor the author assume any responsibility for any injuries or accidents.

To learn more about Cedar Lane Press books, or to find a retailer near you, email info@cedarlanepress.com or visit us at www.cedarlanepress.com.

**PUBLISHER:** Paul McGahren

**EDITORIAL DIRECTOR:** Kerri Grzybicki

**DESIGN:** Lindsay Hess

**DESIGN & LAYOUT:** Chanyn Wise

**PROJECT ILLUSTRATIONS:** Megan Kreiner

**STITCH & TECHNIQUE ILLUSTRATIONS:** Carolyn Mosher

**PHOTOGRAPHER:** Myles Thomas; Magalie Remy (pine-cone and poinsettia on pages 6 and 7)

**TECHNICAL EDITOR:** Tian Connaughton

# *More* CHRISTMAS ORNAMENTS TO CROCHET

## 36 NEW DESIGNS TO CELEBRATE A HANDMADE HOLIDAY

BY MEGAN KREINER

CEDAR LANE PRESS

# CONTENTS

**6**
Introduction

**8**
Tools and Materials

**11**
Crochet Stitches

**14**
Crochet Techniques

**16**
Finishing Stitches

**18**
Ornament Hangers

## 12 DAYS OF CHRISTMAS

Partridge in a Pear Tree .................... 22
Turtle Doves .................................... 26
French Hen ..................................... 30
Calling Bird .................................... 33
Golden Rings ................................... 36
Goose a-Laying ................................ 38
Swan a-Swimming ............................ 41
Maid a-Milking ................................ 44
Lady Dancing .................................. 48
Lord a-Leaping ................................ 52
Piper Piping ................................... 56
Drummer Drumming ........................ 60

## WINTER FLORA

Pinecone ........................................ 66
Holly ............................................. 68
Mistletoe ....................................... 70
Poinsettia ...................................... 72
Christmas Pickle .............................. 74

## THE NUTCRACKER

Sugarplum Fairy .............................. 78
Nutcracker ..................................... 81
Clara ............................................ 86
Mouse King ..................................... 89

## GIFTS FROM SANTA

Train Engine ................................... 94
Puppy in Square Gift Box ................... 99
Kitty in Round Gift Box .................... 103
Rocking Horse ................................ 108
Rag Doll ....................................... 113
Socks .......................................... 116
Lump of Coal ................................. 117

## DECK THE HALLS

Tree Lights ................................... 120
Ringing Bell .................................. 122
Sleigh Bell ................................... 123
Wreath ........................................ 124
Candle ........................................ 126

## PEPPERMINT PALS

Hedgehog ..................................... 130
Rabbit ......................................... 135
Squirrel ....................................... 139

Resources ..................................... **144**
About the Author ............................ **147**
Index .......................................... **148**

# INTRODUCTION

There's something special about the memories connected to the ornaments we choose to hang on a Christmas tree. Happy moments of first Christmases together, new homes, beloved pets, and bobbles lovingly crafted by little hands are hung among evergreen boughs as festive reminders of holidays past, friends and family, vacations abroad, and the joys of childhood. They are beautiful keepsakes of the people, places, and experiences that hold special places in our hearts.

When you crochet a project from this book, you are putting your love and creativity into a very special ornament. From delicate winter flora and traditional yuletide decorations to *The Nutcracker* and "The 12 Days of Christmas," I hope that you'll find the perfect ornament to mark your magical moments and to cherish for many Christmases to come.

Merry Crocheting!

*Megan Kreiner*

by Danielle Atkins

# TOOLS AND MATERIALS

Since the projects in this book require small amounts of yarn and just a few tools to create, it's best to go with quality over quantity. It's always worth using the best-quality materials for your special projects!

## YARN

All of the projects in this book were made using Cascade Heritage 150 sock weight yarn. Please use your favorite brand of sock weight yarn (available online and through your local yarn shop). The yarns used in each project are listed in the resource section (page 146) in the back of this book. If you choose to use yarn of a different weight (such as worsted or chunky) to make toys instead of ornaments, make sure to adjust your hook size accordingly.

## STUFFING

Ornaments are stuffed with polyester fiberfill, which is readily available at most craft stores and will maintain its loft over time.

## CROCHET HOOKS

Crochet hooks come in a variety of materials, sizes, and handle styles. It's ideal if you can hold and try out a hook or two before purchasing. All of the projects in this book were made on a Clover brand Amour hook, size C (2.75 mm). My personal preference is for hooks with ergonomic handles, especially when working with thinner yarns.

For the most accurate sizing, refer to the millimeter measurements when selecting a hook for your project. You can also refer to the chart on page 144 for crochet hook sizes. If you find that your stitches look too loose as you work, try decreasing your hook size.

## NEEDLES

A few steel tapestry needles (size 13 and size 17) are a must for when it's time to assemble your ornaments. Skip the plastic needles as they tend to bend. A size 20 or 22 embroidery or chenille needle is also good for embroidering other details.

In addition to the steel needles, you may also wish to purchase a set of beading needles to apply tiny seed bead details to your completed ornament.

## SCISSORS

When working with yarn and felt, a good pair of fabric or sewing scissors will make for clean cuts and quick snips. I also recommend a small pair of cuticle scissors, which can be helpful and more accurate when cutting out small felt shapes like circles.

## FELT

Craft felt comes in a variety of colors and fiber contents such as polyester, acrylic, wool, and bamboo. Because the felt pieces for ornaments tend to be rather small, it's worth purchasing good quality felt as well-made felt tends to be denser and holds a cleaner edge when cut. When applying felt details to ornaments, I've found that gluing the felt pieces on (and holding them in place with a few marking pins) is often much easier than sewing them in place.

Information about the felts used in this book can be found in the resource section (page 145).

GLUE ON 4 MM PLASTIC EYES WITH LESS MESS! FIRST, DO A DRY FIT FIRST TO GET THE PLACEMENT OF THE EYES JUST RIGHT. PUT A SMALL AMOUNT OF GLUE ON A PIECE OF PAPER. REMOVE ONE EYE AND ROLL THE EYE POST IN THE GLUE. PUSH THE EYE BACK DOWN INTO PLACE AND REPEAT ON THE OTHER EYE.

## PLASTIC EYES

Some of the ornaments in this book call for 4 mm plastic eyes. I like to purchase my plastic eyes online because of the variety of options available. Plastic eyes are often available with sew-on loops or fitted with a plastic post that can be coated with craft glue and inserted into the face of your ornament. In addition to plastic eyes, you can also purchase wire glass eyes or glass beads for your project.

In regards to 4-mm safety eyes, I've found that there are subtle variations in the sizing; sew-on 4-mm eyes run a bit small; 4-mm post eyes with no safety backing are in the middle; and 4-mm safety eyes with a safety backing are a bit bigger.

If plastic eyes are not available to you, you can also try applying French knots in black yarn or embroidery floss, small circles of black felt, or even small dabs of black fabric puff paint.

## JUMP RINGS

Jump rings from 8 mm to 10 mm are small metal rings in various finishes that can be found in the jewelry-making section of your craft store. The rings are sturdy and easy to attach to your finished ornament with just a few stitches.

## CABONE RINGS

Plastic and wooden cabone rings come in a variety of sizes and provide structure for the open circular shapes used in the Partridge in a Pear Tree (page 22), Golden Rings (page 36), Wreath (page 124), and Ringing Bell (page 122) patterns found in this book.

Wooden cabone rings tend to be thicker and rounder than plastic cabone rings. For more information on how to crochet around a cabone ring, see page 15.

## BEADS

Add a little extra sparkle to an ornament by adding a few tiny seed beads with a beading needle and invisible thread. Larger beads can also be used for berries on holly or to decorate ornament hangers (page 19).

To help keep tiny seed beads organized, try using leftover plastic Easter eggs. It's easy to scoop the beads up off the curved sides of the egg with a beading needle and you can close up the egg to store the beads in a pinch.

For tips on creating personalized beads, check out the ornament hanger customizing section on page 19.

## THREAD AND GLUE

To attach seed beads or felt, consider purchasing a spool of "invisible" thread. Invisible thread is a clear plastic filament thread that is clear and is difficult to see. One caveat for the thread is that, because it's clear, it can sometimes be a challenge to work with. I will often put down a piece of white paper and thread a beading needle in front of it so I can see the thread more clearly.

ADD SOME STRENGTH TO YOUR INVISIBLE THREAD BY CUTTING A PIECE TWICE AS LONG AS NEEDED AND FOLDING IT IN HALF. THREAD BOTH ENDS THROUGH YOUR NEEDLE TO CREATE A LARGE LOOP. ONCE YOU'VE DRAWN THE NEEDLE AND DOUBLED UP THREAD THROUGH THE SURFACE OF YOUR WORK, YOU CAN SLIP THE NEEDLE THROUGH THE END OF THE LOOP AND PULL FIRMLY TO SECURE THE THREAD BEFORE YOU START SEWING ON BEADS.

by Danielle Atkins

When gluing on felt and plastic eye details, a general craft glue like Sobo Premium Craft & Fabric Glue works very well. Whichever brand craft glue you choose, make sure it dries clear and goes on fairly thick so it doesn't soak into the yarn fibers before it has a chance to dry.

## PUFF PAINT AND GLITTER

Create a snowy effect on your pinecones (page 66) with white puff paint followed by a dusting of white glitter. Look for fabric paint that is white with a thin applicator tip. Glitter paints tend to dry clear, so look for one that dries white. To give your fabric paint some sparkly, dust the piece with white fine glitter and set aside to set overnight. Shake off the excess glitter once the paint is completely dry. If you make a mistake with your paint, you can wash it off while the paint is still wet, but let your piece dry completely before trying again.

## WIRE AND WIRE TOOLS

Jewelry wire comes in a variety of finishes and can be used for ornament details or for the ornament hangers. A thicker 16 gauge and thinner 20 gauge work well. In addition to the wire, three basic tools are recommended: wire cutters, fine round-nose pliers, and flat (duck bill) pliers.

I found the quality of the wire cutters and pliers improved considerably when I purchased them separately instead of in a jewelry kit. I recommend the Beadsmith and Hakko brands.

For more information on creating ornament hangers, see page 18.

## RIBBONS AND TWINE

Ribbon and colorful twine are widely available in craft stores in a variety of colors and sizes. A simple loop is all you need to hang your ornament on a tree!

When tying and applying bows of ribbon to your ornaments, you can keep the cut edges of your ribbons from fraying with a bit of craft glue. Once the bow is tied, cut the ribbon tails ⅛" to ¼" (3 to 6 mm) longer than needed and apply a light coating of craft glue to just the underside of the ribbon ends with your finger. Allow glue to dry, then trim through the glue-coated ribbon ends.

## NOTIONS AND STORAGE

Here are a few more goodies to add to your ornament-making arsenal!

**Stitch counter:** A row or stitch counter will help you keep track of where you are in your pattern.

**Marking pins:** Super-helpful in positioning your pattern pieces before sewing everything together and for holding glued felt in place as it dries.

**Split or locking rings:** Use these plastic rings to help keep track of the end of your rounds or for when patterns call out for "place markers" (pm) to mark useful landmarks on your work.

**Automatic pencil and sticky notes:** Great for jotting down notes and sticking them into your book as you work.

**Plastic tackle box:** Perfect for organizing a bead collection.

**Project bags:** A small project bag (like a pencil or makeup case) is great for storing smaller tools and notions; a larger bag can hold everything you need for your current project. I find that reusable canvas shopping bags make great project bags!

by Danielle Atkins

# CROCHET STITCHES

Whether you are brand new to crocheting or are a seasoned pro, this section will provide a complete overview of all the stitches used for the patterns in this book as well as some great tips and tricks on how to get the best results out of your work.

## Slipknot

**1** Make a loop with a 6" (15 cm) tail. Overlap the loop on top of the working yarn coming out of the skein.

**2** Insert your hook into the loop and under the working yarn. Gently pull to tighten the yarn around the hook.

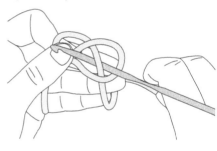

## Yarn Over (YO)

Wrap the yarn over your hook from back to front.

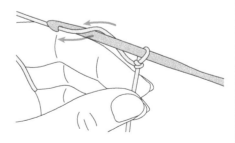

## Chain (ch)

**1** Make a slipknot on your hook.
**2** Yarn over and draw the yarn through the loop on your hook. You will now have 1 loop on your hook with the slipknot below it.

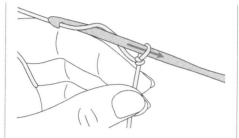

**3** Repeat step 2 until you've made the number of chain stitches specified in the pattern. When checking your chain count, remember that only the chains below the loop on the hook should be counted.

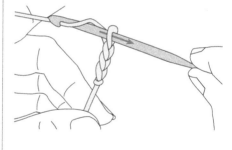

## Slip Stitch (sl st)

Insert your hook into the next chain or stitch. Keep your tension as loose as possible, yarn over, and draw the yarn through the stitch and the loop on your hook.

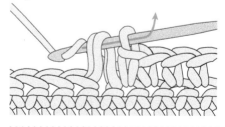

## Single Crochet (sc)

**1** Insert your hook into the next chain or stitch and yarn over. Pull the yarn through the chain or stitch. You will have 2 loops on your hook.

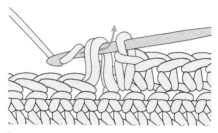

**2** Yarn over and pull yarn through both loops on your hook to complete the single crochet.

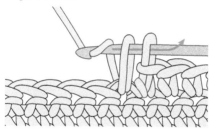

## Half Double Crochet (hdc)

**1** Yarn over and insert your hook into the next chain or stitch. Yarn over a 2nd time and pull the yarn through the chain or stitch. You will have 3 loops on your hook.

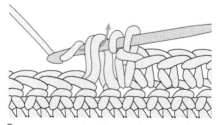

**2** Yarn over and pull yarn through all 3 loops on your hook to complete the half double crochet.

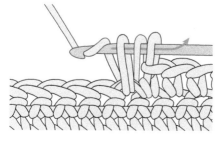

## Double Crochet (dc)

**1** Yarn over and insert your hook into the next chain or stitch. Yarn over a 2nd time and pull the yarn through the chain or stitch. You will have 3 loops on your hook.

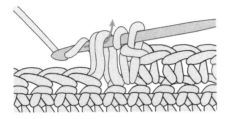

**2** Yarn over and pull yarn through just the first 2 loops on your hook. You will have 2 loops remaining on your hook.

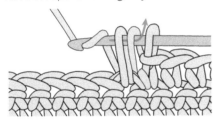

**3** Yarn over and pull yarn through the last 2 loops on your hook to complete the double crochet.

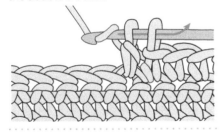

## Treble Crochet (tr)

**1** Yarn over 2 times and insert your hook into the next chain or stitch. Yarn over a 3rd time and pull the yarn through the chain or stitch. You will have 4 loops on your hook.

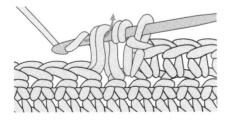

**2** Yarn over and pull yarn through the first 2 loops on your hook. You will have 3 loops remaining on your hook.

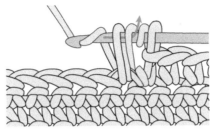

**3** Yarn over and pull yarn through the next 2 loops on your hook. You will have 2 loops remaining on your hook.

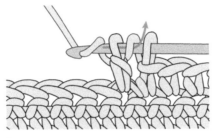

**4** Yarn over and pull yarn through the remaining 2 loops on your hook to finish the treble crochet.

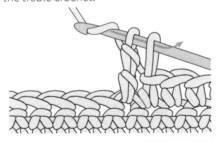

## Front Post Single Crochet (FPsc)

**1** Insert your hook below your next stitch to the right of the stitch's post. Work the hook around the post from front to back to front again and yarn over.

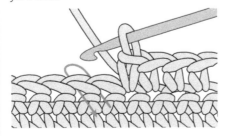

**2** Pull the yarn around the back of the post. You will have 2 loops on your hook. Yarn over and pull yarn through both loops on your hook to finish the stitch.

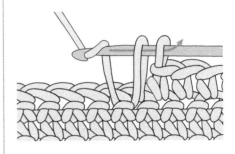

## Back Post Single Crochet (BPsc)

**1** Starting behind your work, insert your hook below your next stitch to the right of the stitch's post. Work the hook around the post from back to front to back again and yarn over.

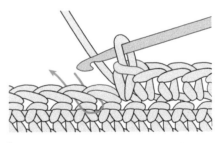

**2** Pull the yarn around the front of the post. You will have 2 loops on the hook. Yarn over and pull yarn through both loops on the hook to finish the stitch.

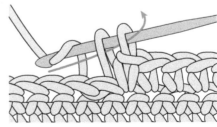

You can also work around the post using other stitches like half double crochet (FPhdc/BPhdc) or double crochet (FPdc/BPdc).

## Increases (sc 2 in next st)

Work 2 or more stitches into the same stitch when indicated.

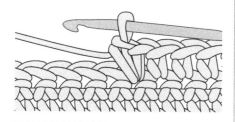

## Decreases

Patterns in this book use a variety of decrease options, such as crocheting 2 to 3 stitches together and/or skipping stitches entirely.

## Skip (sk)

Per the pattern instructions, count and skip the number of stitches indicated before working the next stitch in the pattern.

## Single-Crochet Decrease (sc2tog)

**1** Insert your hook into the next stitch, yarn over the hook, and pull through the stitch, leaving a loop on your hook. You'll have 2 loops on your hook.
**2** Repeat step 1 in the next stitch. You'll have 3 loops on your hook.
**3** Yarn over the hook and pull through all 3 loops. You'll have 1 loop on your hook.

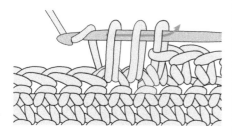

## Half-Double Crochet Decrease (Hdc2tog)

Yarn over first and then proceed to step 1. You will have 3 loops on your hook. Yarn over again and proceed to step 2. You will have 5 loops on your hook. Yarn over and pull yarn through all loops on hook to complete the decrease.

## Double Crochet Decrease (dc2tog)

Yarn over first and then proceed to step 1. You will have 3 loops on your hook. Yarn over again and proceed to step 2. You will have 5 loops on your hook. Yarn over and pull yarn through the first 4 loops on hook so 2 loops remain. Yarn over and pull yarn through remaining 2 loops to complete the decrease.

## Single Crochet 3 Together (sc3tog)

Keep repeating step 2 until you have 4 loops on your hook. Proceed to yarn over and pull the hook through all loops to complete the decrease.

## Single Crochet 4 Together (sc4tog)

Keep repeating step 2 until you have 5 loops on your hook. Proceed to yarn over and pull the hook through all loops to complete the decrease.

## Invisible Single-Crochet Decrease (sc2tog)

This technique can be used instead of the standard single-crochet decrease. It helps eliminate the gaps that can sometimes occur when using the standard single-crochet decrease.
**1** Insert your hook into the front loop of the next stitch and then immediately into the front loop of the following stitch. You will have 3 loops on your hook.

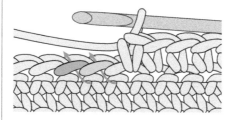

**2** Yarn over and draw the working yarn through the 2 front loops on the hook. You'll have 2 loops on your hook.

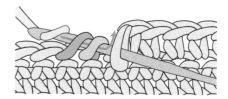

**3** Yarn over the hook and pull through both loops on your hook to complete the stitch. You'll have 1 loop on your hook.

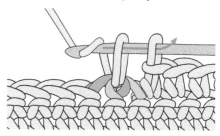

For an invisible half double crochet decrease (hdc2tog), yarn over first and then proceed to decrease as written for the single-crochet decrease until you have 3 loops on your hook. Yarn over and draw through all 3 loops to complete the stitch.

## Working in Back Loops (bl), Front Loops (fl), and Both Loops (tbl)

Unless otherwise noted, work in both loops of a stitch except when the pattern instructs that a stitch should be worked in the back loop or front loop. The front loop is the loop closest to you. The back loop is behind the front loop. If a round or row begins with "In bl" or "In fl," work entire round/row in that manner unless you are instructed to switch.

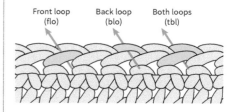

Front loop (flo)    Back loop (blo)    Both loops (tbl)

# CROCHET TECHNIQUES

## Working in Rows

Work the pattern until you reach the end of the row. Turn your work. Before beginning the next row, you will be asked to make a turning chain per the pattern instructions. Once your chain is completed, skip the turning chain and insert your hook into the first stitch in your new row and continue working the pattern.

## Working in the Round

Many patterns in this book are worked in a spiral round in which there are no slip stitches or chains between rounds. When you reach the end of the round, simply continue crocheting into the next. If needed, use a place marker to keep track of where your rounds begin and end.

## Adjustable Ring (AR)

The adjustable ring is a great technique that will minimize the hole in the middle of your starting round.

**1** Form a ring with your yarn, leaving a 6" (15 cm) tail. Insert the hook into the loop as if you were making a slipknot.

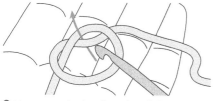

**2** Yarn over the hook and pull through the loop to make a slip stitch, but do not tighten the loop.

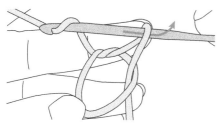

**3** Chain 1 and then single crochet over both strands of yarn that make up the edge of the adjustable ring until you've reached the number of stitches indicated in the pattern. To close the center of the ring, pull firmly on the yarn tail.

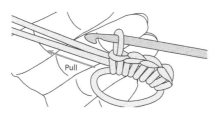

To start your next round, work your next stitch in the first single crochet of the completed adjustable ring. For patterns that require a semi-circle base shape, you will be asked to turn the work so that the back of the piece faces you before you make a turning chain and begin working the next row in your pattern.

## Working in a Chain Space (ch sp)

Proceed with making your next stitch as you normally would, but work your stitches into the space below the chain.

## Right Side (RS)/Wrong Side (WS)

When working in the round, the side of your pattern perceived as the "right side" will affect which part of the stitch is the back loop versus the front loop. The 6" (15 cm) tail left over from forming the adjustable ring will usually be on the wrong side of the piece. The same can be said for patterns that begin by working around a chain, provided you hold the 6" (15 cm) yarn tail at the back of your work as you crochet the first round.

## Changing Colors

Work the stitch up to the last step where you would normally draw the yarn through the loop(s) on your hook to complete the stitch. To change colors, yarn over the hook with your new color and draw it through the remaining loop(s) on your hook, completing the stitch. Continue on to the next stitch in the new color.

For color changes at the beginning of a new row, complete the stitch in your previous row and turn your work. Introduce the new color when you make your turning chain. Continue to work with your new color for the next row.

For color changes that take place in a slip stitch, simply insert the hook into the old color stitch, yarn over with the new color, and draw the new color through the loop on your hook to complete your slip stitch and the color change.

## Working Around a Chain

When working around a chain of stitches, first work in the back ridge loops of the chain and then in the front side to create your first round.

**1** Make a chain per the pattern instructions. To begin round 1, work your first stitch in the back ridge loop of the 2nd chain from your hook. Mark this stitch to make it easier to find when you are ready to begin round 2. Work the rest of the stitches indicated into the back ridge loops until you've reached the last chain above the slipknot. Work the indicated number of stitches into the back ridge loop of this last chain.

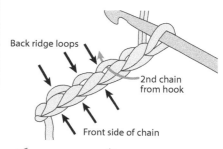

Back ridge loops

2nd chain from hook

Front side of chain

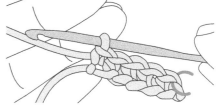

**2** To work the other side of the chain, rotate your work so the front side of the chain faces up. Starting in the next chain, insert the hook under the front side of the chain to work the next stitch.

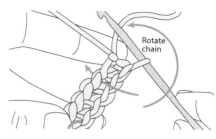

**3** Continue working in the front sides of the remaining chains. Once the round is complete, continue on to round 2 (indicated by your stitch marker).

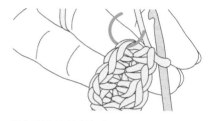

## Surface Loops

Working in just the front or back loop creates a line of surface loops. These lines of raised stitches serve as landmarks when bending your work and will usually remain visible on the right side of the work. Look for references to surface loops on assembly illustrations represented by a line of closely spaced stitches.

## Working in Surface Stitches

Some patterns have details created by crocheting into the surface of specific stitches, like working surface stitches into the raised loops that become visible after working into back loops or front posts of a previous round. Orient your work as the pattern indicates so the additional rounds of surface stitches will lay properly against your work.

**1** Locate the round to work in. Insert the hook under the exposed loop(s) on the surface. Rejoin yarn with a yarn over and pull yarn through surface stitch.

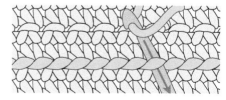

Exposed front loops from working bl sc sts

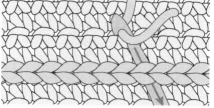

Exposed loops from working FPsc sts

**2** Chain 1 and apply a stitch (like a single crochet) into the same surface loop you started in. This will create your first surface stitch.

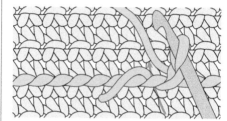

You can then continue to work in the remaining surface stitches in the round.

## Twisted Cords

Cut a length of yarn 4 to 6 times longer than your finished cord will be. Holding the cut ends in one hand, take the folded end in your other hand and catch the loop on your finger. Spin/rotate your finger to twist the yarn.

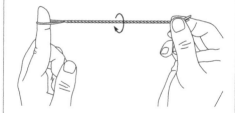

Continue to twist until the yarn twists and doubles over on itself. Measure out the final length of cord needed and tie the folded and cut ends together in a square knot to secure the twist.

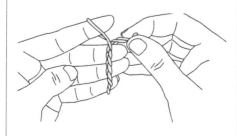

## Covering a Cabone Ring

**1** To cover the cabone ring with single crochet stitches, make a slip knot and place the loop above the knot on your hook. Hold the hook and slip knot against the front side of the ring with the working yarn draped over the top. Reach the hook through the center of the ring, yarn over, and pull the yarn through to the front. You'll have two loops on your hook.

**2** Hold the hook above the top edge of the ring, yarn over, and draw the yarn through the two loops on your hook to make your first st around the cabone ring.

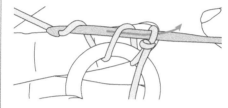

**3** Reach the hook through the ring, yarn over, and pull a loop through. You'll have two loops on your hook.

**4** Hold the hook above the top ring edge, yarn over, and draw the yarn through the two loops on your hook to complete the stitch. Repeat steps 3 and 4.

### MAKE QUICK WORK OF YOUR YARN TAIL AT THE START OF YOUR RING!

Hold your yarn tail against your cabone ring and crochet around both the ring and the yarn tail for the first 5 to 10 stitches so you can secure and trim the yarn tail off when done.

# FINISHING STITCHES

Once your pattern pieces are complete, you can assemble and embellish your ornaments with just a handful of basic stitches. To ensure all the final details end up in the right spots, look over the photos for each ornament before you begin assembling them and use marking pins to help you work out the placement of your pattern pieces before sewing them together.

Leave long yarn tails when you fasten off the last rounds of your arm and leg pieces. When assembling, use marking pins to attach all your limbs to the body to ensure everything is even and balanced. Then, using the leftover yarn tails, place a single stitch at each marking pin to hold your pieces in place. Remove the pins and finish sewing your pieces down using a whip or mattress stitch.

## Whip Stitch

Use this stitch to close flat seams. Hold the edges of your work together and, using your tapestry needle and yarn, draw the yarn through the edges before looping the yarn over the top of your work and back through the edges again in a spiral-like motion. Continue until the seam is closed or the piece is attached.

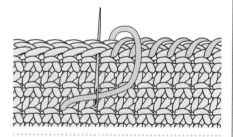

## Mattress Stitch

The mattress stitch provides a nice tight seam when sewing crochet surfaces together, like a head to the open edges of a neck.

Choose a point on the surface or edge of your first piece and insert the needle from A to B under a single stitch and pull the yarn through. Cross over to the opposite surface and draw your needle under a single stitch from C to D with the entry point at C lining up between points A and B on the first

surface. Return to the first surface and insert your needle directly next to exit point B. Continue to work back and forth in this manner until seam is closed, pulling firmly after every few stitches to ensure a clean, closed seam.

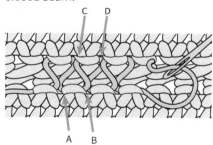

## Long Stitch

Use this stitch to help shape the surface of your ornament. With your yarn and tapestry needle, draw the yarn up through the surface of your piece (1) and then reinsert the needle in a different location (2). Repeat if desired to double or triple up the yarn. To cinch the surface of your piece for details like toes or lip clefts, pull the yarn firmly as you work.

Up at 1, down at 2.

## Closing Round Holes

For closing round holes like the ones at the last rounds of heads and body shapes, start by threading the remaining yarn tail onto a tapestry needle. Following the edge of the round opening, insert the needle through just the front loops of each stitch, effectively winding the yarn tail around the front loops of the stitches. When you've worked all the way around the opening, pull the tail firmly to close the hole (just like you were cinching a drawstring bag closed).

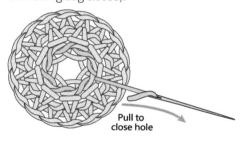

Pull to close hole

## Running Stitch

Use this stitch to attach felt pieces or flattened crochet pieces to your work. To apply this stitch, draw your yarn or thread in and out of the surface(s) of your piece in a dashed line pattern.

## Satin Stitch

Apply satin stitches by grouping short- or medium-length stitches closely together to build up a shape or fill an area with color.

## Chain Stitch

**1** Start by making a small stitch on the surface of your work. Bring the needle up through your work about a stitch length away, pass the needle through the small stitch, and reinsert the needle into its starting point. This is your first chain.

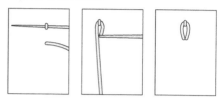

**2** Bring your needle up through your work a stitch below your last chain. Slide the needle under your last chain and reinsert the needle into its starting point. Repeat.

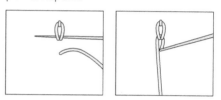

## Lazy Daisy/Overcast Stitch

This stitch can be adjusted to create tight petal shapes or wider curved shapes like eyebrows or mouths. Begin by drawing the yarn up through the surface of your piece at (A) and then reinsert the needle at (B), leaving the yarn loose to achieve the desired level of curve. Choose a point along the curved long stitch and draw up the yarn at (C) and reinsert at (D) to hold the shape of the long stitch in place. Feel free to repeat if desired at other points along the long stitch if needed.

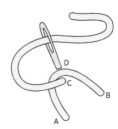

### DOES YOUR ORNAMENT'S HAIR OR FUR NEED A BIT OF TAMING?!

A bit of soft-hold hair gel can give you just a bit more control of your character's coif! Apply a bit of hair gel to your fingers and add a thin coat to the yarn. Pose and shape the hair or fur to your liking and allow it to dry. Before styling, it is highly recommended that you test your gels on a bit of scrap yarn before applying it to your finished ornament.

## Couching

This technique involves sewing down piece of thicker yarn running along the top of the surface of your work with a thinner thread. Place and pose your yarn on the surface of your work, then use a needle and thread to intermittently sew a stitch over the yarn to hold its shaping in place. This stitch can be used to create effects like piped icing on cookies.

### TRY THIS TRICK TO REDUCE THE HASSLE OF DEALING WITH YARN ENDS WHEN ADDING EMBROIDERY DETAILS!

Begin by inserting your needle about an inch from where you intend to start your embroidery and leave a 4" (10 cm) tail. Bring the needle up at the first stitch. Hold the yarn tail down with your fingers as you work the first couple of stitches until the yarn appears to feel secure. When you finish your last stitch, bring the needle out at the same spot of the beginning tail and cut the end, leaving another 4" (10 cm) tail. Knot the yarn tails together, then use a crochet hook or tapestry needle to draw the yarn and the knot back through the hole with a firm tug. Trim any visible yarn tails if needed.

## Fringe Knots

Add a little hair to your character! Insert your hook through a surface stitch on your work and fold a 4" piece of yarn over the hook. Draw the yarn halfway through the surface stitch to create a small loop. Proceed to pull the loose ends of the yarn through this loop and pull tightly to secure it. For a fuzzier look, use a steel tapestry needle to separate the yarn plys and fluff them with your fingers or a fine toothed comb. Trim as needed.

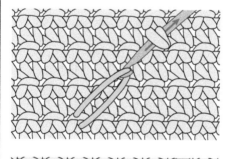

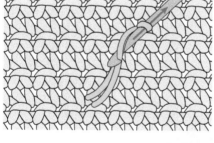

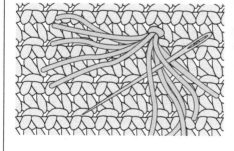

by Danielle Collins

# ORNAMENT HANGERS

Beautiful ornaments deserve special hangers. With just a few simple wire-working tools, some beads, and a couple of spools of jewelry wire, your ornaments can be hanging pretty on a lovely set of custom hooks.

RIBBON AND TWINE MAKE LOVELY HANGING LOOPS FOR ORNAMENTS AS WELL! YOU CAN EVEN SLIP A FEW BEADS ONTO A LOOP OF RIBBON AND SECURE THEM WITH A KNOT.

After you attach the jump ring to your ornament, thread ribbon or twine through the ring and tie the ends in a bow. To keep the bow ends from fraying, cut the ends of the ribbons ⅛" to ¼" (3 to 6 mm) longer than needed and apply a light coating of craft glue to just the underside of the ribbon ends with your finger. Allow glue to dry, then trim the glue-coated ribbon ends to their final length.

## GETTING STARTED

To create your own wire hangers, you will need the following tools and materials.

*   Wire cutters (Hakko recommended)
*   Fine round-nose pliers  (Beadsmith recommended)
*   Flat/duck bill pliers (Beadsmith recommended)
*   Jewelry wire (16 gauge)
*   Jewelry wire (20 gauge)
*   Assorted beads
*   8 mm–10 mm jump rings

## PRACTICE MAKES PERFECT

If you are new to working with wire (like I was when I started this chapter), it's likely your first 2, 3, or 10 hangers may not be perfect. It takes practice, like anything else!

## ATTACH A JUMP RING

Give your ornament a sturdy hanging point by sewing a jump ring onto the surface of your work. To check your hanging point before you attach the jump ring, hook the point where you want to attach your jump ring with your needle or crochet hook and allow your work to be suspended on the needle or hook to see how it balances (and whether you need to adjust that location).

## WIRE BENDING TIPS

For the larger "Simple," "Crook," and "Headpin" hangers, cut a piece of 16-gauge wire to the length suggested on the template you wish to follow. Begin by creating one of the loops at the end of the wire by holding the end in your round-nose pliers and bending the wire around the pliers (versus twisting the pliers to bend the wire). Once you have your loop, hold the wire with your flat/duck bill pliers and gently bend the wire with your fingers.

Chances are, you will end up with some sharp and bumpy crimp points in the wires' curves as you work. Leave them for now and focus on getting the general shape. Once the main curves are in, trim off any excess and use round-nose pliers to bend the loop at the other end of the wire.

To smooth out your crimps and reshape your curves, draw your flat/duck bill pliers over the problem areas, clamping the pliers up and down as you move to reshape

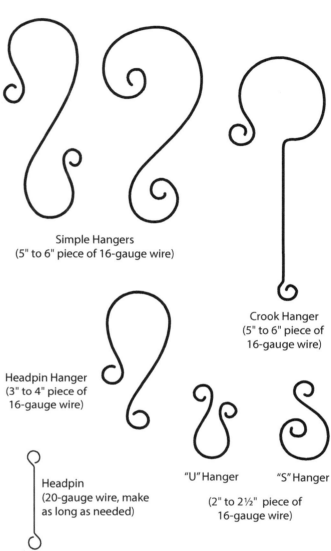

Simple Hangers
(5" to 6" piece of 16-gauge wire)

Crook Hanger
(5" to 6" piece of
16-gauge wire)

Headpin Hanger
(3" to 4" piece of
16-gauge wire)

Headpin
(20-gauge wire, make
as long as needed)

"U" Hanger

"S" Hanger

(2" to 2½" piece of
16-gauge wire)

and smooth out the wire. Lay the hanger on top of the template to check the shape as you work. Keep on clamping and moving over the wire until you are happy with the shape.

For the beaded section of the headpin hanger, cut a length of 20-gauge wire and straighten it out. Bend a loop on one end. Thread beads onto the headpin. Cut the remaining wire to roughly ⅜" (9 mm) from the last bead and twist the end into a loop with your round-nose pliers to secure beads.

For the Crook hanger, thread beads onto the straight section of the hanger. Cut the remaining wire to roughly ⅜" (9 mm) from the last bead and twist the end into a loop to secure beads. With flat pliers, twist the loop at the bottom of the crook so it is perpendicular to the rest of the hanger.

For the smaller "U" and "S" hangers, apply the small loops to both ends of the wire before bending the wire into its final shape. They can then be added as the bottom link on the Headpin and Crook hangers.

## CUSTOMIZING AND PERSONALIZING

Try customizing the beads on your hanger with a date or monogram to celebrate a special event.

To customize wooden beads, you will need:
- 20 mm wooden coin beads (available on Etsy and online bead stores)
- Oil-based metallic extra-fine paint pens
- Number and/or letter stickers

**Stickers:** Consider bringing your beads with you when picking out stickers (so you know they will fit). Stickers can also be applied to a variety of other bead shapes and materials, so let your imagination run wild!

**Metallic Paint Pens:** When using paint pens, the metallic extra-fine type seems to bleed less than the white one. Trace your bead onto a sheet of paper and practice what you want to paint before you begin.

When painting on the surface of a wooden coin bead, keep an eye out for rough surfaces that might cause the paint to bleed when applied. Mistakes can be mostly wiped away if done quickly while the paint is still wet. To hide a mistake, consider covering the wiped side with a sticker and redo lettering on the other side of the bead.

Here's a few more ideas to customize your ornament hangers:
- Custom punched copper tags from Etsy
- Bakeable clay, such as Sculpey. **Option 1:** Roll out beads, flatten the surface, and run them through with a toothpick before you stamp with solvent-type ink and bake. **Option 2:** Flatten out a sheet of clay, stamp with solvent-type ink, cut out the bead, bake, and then drill a hole.
- Chipboard or chalk board gift tags with glittery stickers

# 12 DAYS OF CHRISTMAS

*I* was doing a bit of research on the "12 Days of Christmas" song before putting the patterns together for this chapter and was delighted to discover some alternative gifts my true love could have sent to me. These offerings included "ships a-sailing," "hounds a-running," "badgers baiting," and, my personal favorite, "asses racing" from a 1905 version.

If you have your heart set on adding some racing donkeys to your 12 Days of Christmas collection, you can find an adorable donkey pattern in my first volume of *Christmas Ornaments to Crochet*.

# PARTRIDGE IN A PEAR TREE

······ DIFFICULTY: INTERMEDIATE * FINISHED SIZE: 3 1/2" TALL, 2 1/2" WIDE (9 X 6 CM)·······

## ⇌ MATERIALS ⇌

- Sock weight yarn in black, brown, gold, gray, green, ivory, orange, red, and tan
- Hook size C (2.75 mm)
- (2) 4 mm plastic safety eyes
- Craft glue or needle and thread
- (1) 2" (5 cm) plastic cabone ring
- Polyester fiberfill
- Tapestry needle
- Scissors
- (1) 8–10 mm jump ring
- Place marker

## BODY

With ivory yarn, make a 6-st adjustable ring.

**Rnd 1:** Sc 2 in each st around. (12 sts)

**Rnd 2:** *Sc 1, sc 2 in next st; rep from * 5 more times. (18 sts)

Cut ivory yarn. Change to gray.

**Rnds 3–4:** Sc 18.

**Rnd 5:** Sc 8, change to ivory, sc 2, change to gray, sc 8. (18 sts)

**Rnd 6:** Sc 1, sc2tog 3 times, change to ivory, sc 4, change to gray, sc2tog 3 times, sc 1. (12 sts)

Cut gray. Change to ivory.

**Rnd 7:** *Sc 2, sc 2 in next st; rep from * 3 more times. (16 sts)

**Rnd 8:** Sc 16.

**Rnd 9:** *Sc 2, sc2tog; rep from * 3 more times. (12 sts)

**Rnd 10:** *Sc 1, sc2tog; rep from * 3 more times. (8 sts)

Fasten off, stuff body, close hole, and weave in end.

## BACK AND TAIL

With tan, ch 5.

**Row 1:** Working in back ridge loops of ch, sc 2 in 2nd ch from hook, sc 2, sc 3 in next ch. Rotate ch so front loops of ch are facing up. Starting in next ch and working in front loops, sc 2, sc 2 in next ch, ch 1, turn. (11 sts)

**Row 2:** Sk ch 1, sc 2 in next 2 sts, hdc 2, sc 2 in next st, sc 1, sc 2 in next st, hdc 2, sc 2 in next 2 sts, ch 1, turn. (17 sts)

**Row 3:** Sk ch 1, sc 2 in next st, hdc 4, sc 7, hdc 4, sc 2 in next st, ch 1, turn. (19 sts)

**Row 4:** Sk ch 1, sc 1, pm, sc 5, sk 1, sl st 1, sc 1, (hdc 1, ch 2, sl st in back ridge loop of 2nd ch from hook, hdc 1) in next st, sc 1, sl st 1, sk 1, sc 6. Do not turn.

# PARTRIDGE IN A PEAR TREE (continued)

## TAIL DETAIL

**Rnd 5:** Ch 3 and work across the gap to marked st in row 4. Sc in pm st and work 5 more sc sts across the raw edge of the work. Cont to work the tail in the rnd. (9 sts)

**Rnd 6:** Sc 4 into ch-3 sp, sc 6. (10 sts)

**Rnd 7:** *Sc 4, sc 2 in next st; rep from * 1 more time. (12 sts)

**Rnd 8:** Sc 12.

**Rnd 9:** *Sc 1, sc2tog; rep from * 3 more times. (8 sts)

Fasten off yarn, flatten end of tail, and whip stitch seam closed.

Wrap back and tail piece over the back of the body with the pointy "peak" detail from row 4 in the middle of the fore-head (lined up over the white "peak" detail on the chest). Pin and sew down edges. Sew the open edge of tail to rnd 3 at the base to body.

With black yarn, embroider a ch stitch around the white portion of the face. With orange yarn, sew satin stitches to the front of face for a beak. Glue 4 mm plastic eyes on either side of the beak.

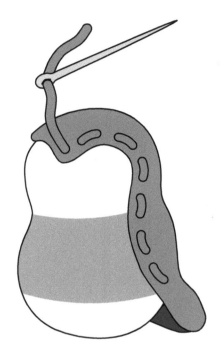

## WING (MAKE 2)

With tan, make a 6-st adjustable ring.

**Rnd 1:** Sc 2 in next 2 sts, (sc 1, hdc 1) in next st, (hdc 1, ch 2, sl st in base of ch 2, hdc 1) in next st, (hdc 1, sc 1) in next st, sc 2 in next st.

With the round edges of the wings facing forward, whip stitch the top edge of the wings to the shoulders of the bird. Leave the bottom and back edges of the wings loose.

With brown yarn, make a small loop at the top of the head. Wind and secure the yarn around the base of the loop 2 to 3 times and fasten off.

## PEAR (MAKE 4)

With gold yarn, make a 4-st adjustable ring.

**Rnd 1:** Sc 2 in each st around. (8 sts)

**Rnd 2:** Sc 8.

**Rnd 3:** *Sc 2, sc2tog; rep from * 1 more time. (6 sts)

Stuff pear.

**Rnd 4:** *Sc 1, sc2tog; rep from * 1 more time. (4 sts)

Fasten off, close hole, and weave in end.

Attach (1) 6" (15 cm) piece of brown yarn to the bottom of the pear. Draw yarn up through the top of the pear for a stem. Tie a knot at the base of the stem, then trim stem short.

## TREE LEAF RING

With green, (sl st, ch 1) around the 2" (5 cm) plastic cabone ring.

**Rnd 1:** Sc around the entire edge of the ring until ring is fully covered (50 to 60 sts).

**Rnd 2:** *(Sl st, ch-3, sk ch 3, sl st) in next st, sk 1; rep from * until 4 sts remain. Fasten off.

## POT AND TRUNK

With red yarn, make a 5-st adjustable ring.

**Rnd 1:** Sc 2 in each st around. (10 sts)

**Rnd 2:** BPsc 10.

**Rnds 3–4:** Sc 10.

**Rnd 5:** In bl, *sc 3, sc2tog; rep from * 1 more time. (8 sts)

Cut red yarn. Change to brown.

**Rnd 6:** FPsc 8.

Lightly stuff pot.

**Rnd 7:** *Sc 2, sc2tog; rep from * 1 more time. (6 sts)

**Rnds 8–9:** Sc 6.

Fasten off.

## POT RIM DETAIL

**Rnd 1:** With pot pointed up and using red yarn, (sl st 1, ch 1, sc 1) in one of the rnd 6 exposed fl. Cont to work 7 more sc sts into the fl of rnd 6. (8 sts)

**Rnd 2:** Sl st 8.

Fasten off, leaving a long tail for sewing.

To help flatten the bottom of the pot, draw the leftover yarn tail from the interior of the pot rim down through the

bottom of the pot and back up the interior of the rim 2 to 3 times and tie off.

Attach the open edge of the trunk to the 4-st space at the bottom of the tree leaf ring.

Place the bird in the center of the tree leaf ring and secure with a few stitches in green. Attach four pears to the lower half of the tree leaf ring.

Sew on a jump ring. Add a hanger (page 18).

# TURTLE DOVES

····· DIFFICULTY: INTERMEDIATE * FINISHED SIZE: 2 1/2" TALL, 3 1/2" WIDE (6 X 9 CM)·······

## ⇌ MATERIALS ⇌

- Sock weight yarn in black, dark gray, ivory, light gray, and rose
- Hook size C (2.75 mm)
- (1) 3 1/2" (9 cm) twig
- (4) 4 mm plastic safety eyes
- Craft glue or needle and thread
- Polyester fiberfill
- Tapestry needle
- Scissors
- (1) 8–10 mm jump ring

## BODY AND HEAD (MAKE 2)

With ivory yarn, make an 8-st adjustable ring.

**Rnd 1:** Sc 2 in each st around. (16 sts)

**Rnd 2:** *Sc 1, sc 2 in next st; rep from * 7 more times. (24 sts)

**Rnds 3–4:** Sc 24.

**Rnd 5:** *Sc 4, sc2tog; rep from * 3 more times. (20 sts)

**Cut ivory yarn. Change to rose.**

**Rnd 6:** Sc 20.

Cut rose yarn. Change to light gray.

**Rnd 7:** *Sc 3, sc2tog; rep from * 3 more times. (16 sts)

**Rnd 8:** Sc2tog 2 times, sc 8, sc2tog 2 times. (12 sts)

**Rnd 9:** *Sc 2, sc 2 in next st; rep from * 3 more times. (16 sts)

**Rnds 10–11:** Sc 16.

**Stuff body.**

**Rnd 12:** Sc2tog 8 times. (8 sts)

Stuff head, close hole, and fasten off.

## BACK AND TAIL (MAKE 2)

With light gray yarn, ch 4.

**Row 1:** Working in back ridge loops of ch, sc 2 in 2nd ch from hook, sc 1, sc 4 in next ch. Rotate ch so front loops of ch are facing up. Starting in next ch and working in front loops, sc 1, sc 2 in next ch, ch 1, turn. (10 sts)

**Row 2:** Sk ch 1, sc 2 in next 2 sts, hdc 1, sc 2 in next st, sc 2, sc 2 in next st, hdc 1, sc 2 in next 2 sts, ch 1, turn. (16 sts)

**Row 3:** Sk ch 1, sc 2 in next st, hdc 4, sc 6, hdc 4, sc 2 in next st, ch 1, turn. (18 sts)

**Row 4:** Sk ch 1, sc 1, pm, sc 5, sc 3 in next st, sl st 4, sc 3 in next st, sc 6. Do not turn.

## TAIL DETAIL

**Rnd 5:** Ch 3 and work across the gap to marked st in row 4. Sc in marked st and work 6 more sc across the raw edge of the work. Cont to work the tail in the rnd. (7 sts)

# TURTLE DOVES *(continued)*

**Rnd 6:** Sc 3 into ch-3 sp, sc 7. (10 sts)

**Rnd 7:** *Sc 4, sc 2 in next st; rep from * 1 more time. (12 sts)

**Rnd 8:** *Sc 5, sc 2 in next st; rep from * 1 more time. (14 sts)

Cut light gray yarn. Change to black.

**Rnds 9–10:** Sc 14.

Fasten off, flatten end of tail, and whip stitch seam closed.

Line up top of back and tail with rnd 8 of the body. Wrap back and tail over the back half of the body. Pin and sew down edges. Sew the open inner edge of tail to the base of the body, adding a small bit of stuffing to tail before closing seam.

Rep on 2nd bird.

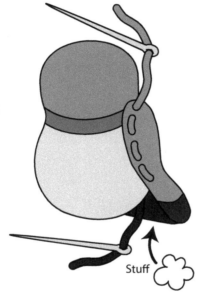

Stuff

## BEAK (MAKE 2)

With dark gray yarn, make a 3-st adjustable ring. Fasten off in center of adjustable ring.

Attach beak to the front of the face with rounded edge facing out.

With ivory yarn, ch 3 and fasten off. Drape the ch-3 over the top of the beak and attach the beg and end of the ch to the sides of the beak.

With black yarn, apply 2 curved short stitches on either side of the beak for closed eyes. Using a single yarn ply from your black yarn or black embroidery thread, apply 1 short stitch above each eye for an eyebrow.

With black yarn, sew a set of 3 parallel lines to sides of the head behind the eyes. With white yarn, apply 2 lines in between the 3 black lines.

Rep on 2nd bird.

## WING (MAKE 4)

With light gray yarn, make a 7-st adjustable ring.

**Rnd 1:** Sc 2 in next 3 sts, (hdc 1, dc 1, hdc 1) in next st, sc 2 in next 3 sts. (15 sts)

**Rnd 2:** Sc 2, sc 2 in next 2 sts, change to black, hdc 3, (hdc 1, dc 1, hdc 1) in next st, hdc 3, change to light gray, sc 2 in next 2 sts, sc 2. (21 sts)

Fasten off, leaving a long yarn tail for sewing.

Hold wing horizontal. Fold the top third of the wing back and tack shaping down with a few light gray stitches. Rep fold in the opposite direction for the other wing. With the folds pressed against the sides of the body, sew the upper half of the wings to the shoulders and upper back of the body. Sew the tips of the wings down to the lower back of the body.

Rep on 2nd bird.

## FEET

Cut (1) 3½" (9 cm) twig. Double up dark gray yarn on a tapestry needle. Hold the left side of the stick against the lower belly of one bird and loop the yarn around the stick 3 to 4 times, catching the underside of the belly as you sew to create a foot. Rep 1 more time to create the other foot. Rep on the right side of the stick with the other bird.

Tilt the bird heads tog so they touch. With light gray yarn, sew the heads tog at the point where they touch with a few stitches.

Sew on a jump ring. Add a hanger (page 18).

# FRENCH HEN

······· DIFFICULTY: INTERMEDIATE * FINISHED SIZE: 2 1/2" TALL, 3 1/2" LONG (6 X 9 CM) ·······

## ⇌ MATERIALS ⇌

- Sock weight yarn in black, dark purple, gold, green, blue, light purple, magenta, red, and tan
- Hook size C (2.75 mm)
- (2) 4 mm plastic safety eyes
- Craft glue or needle and thread
- Polyester fiberfill
- Tapestry needle
- Scissors
- (1) 8–10 mm jump ring
- Place marker

## BODY

With dark purple, ch 5.

**Rnd 1:** Starting in 2nd ch from hook and working in back ridge loops, sc 3, sc 5 back ridge loop of next ch. Rotate ch so front loops are facing up. Starting in next ch and working in front loops, sc 2, sc 2 in fl of next ch. (12 sts)

**Rnd 2:** Sc 2 in next st, sc 2, hdc 2 in next 5 sts, sc 2, sc 2 in next 2 sts. (20 sts)

**Rnd 3:** Sc 2 in next 2 sts, sc 4, hdc 2 in next 6 sts, sc 4, sc 2 in next 4 sts. (32 sts)

**Rnds 4–10:** Sc 32.

**Rnd 11:** *Sc 6, sc2tog; rep from * 3 more times. (28 sts)

**Rnd 12:** *Sc 5, sc2tog; rep from * 3 more times. (24 sts)

Fasten off yarn and stuff body. Flatten seam horizontally at the back of the body and whip stitch closed.

## HEAD

With gold yarn, make an 8-st adjustable ring.

**Rnd 1:** *Sc 1, sc 2 in next st; rep from * 3 more times. (12 sts)

**Rnds 2–4:** Sc 12.

**Rnd 5:** *Sc 2, sc 2 in next st; rep from * 3 more times. (16 sts)

**Rnd 6:** *Sc 1, sc 2 in next st; rep from * 7 more times. (24 sts)

**Rnd 7:** BPsc 24.

Cut gold, leaving a 48" (122 cm) tail.

Change to magenta.

**Rnd 8:** *Sc 3, sc 2 in next st; rep from * 5 more times. (30 sts)

**Rnd 9:** BPsc 30.

Cut magenta, leaving a 48" (122 cm) tail.

Change to light purple.

**Rnd 10:** *Hdc 1, ch 2, hdc 1, sl st 1; rep from * 9 more times. (30 sts)

Draw out the magenta yarn tail. Working in the exposed front loops from rnd 9, *sl st 1, hdc 1, ch 2, hdc 1; rep from * to end.

Draw out the gold yarn tail. Working in the exposed front loops from rnd 7, *sl st 1, hdc 1, ch 2, hdc 1; rep from * 7 more times.

Stuff head and sew to top front of body (above the hdc sts in rnds 2 and 3 of body).

Stuff

## WING (MAKE 2)

With magenta yarn, make a 7-st adjustable ring.

**Rnd 1:** Sc 2 in next 3 sts, (hdc 1, dc 1, hdc 1) in next st, sc 2 in next 3 sts. (15 sts)

**Rnd 2:** Sc 2, sc 2 in next 2 sts, hdc 3, (hdc 1, dc 1, hdc 1) in next st, hdc 3, sc 2 in next 2 sts, sc 2. (21 sts)

**Cut magenta yarn. Change to light purple.**

### Left wing

**Rnd 3:** Sl st 6, (sc 1, ch 2, sc 1) in next 5 sts, sl st 10. Fasten off.

### Right wing

**Rnd 3:** Sl st 10, (sc 1, ch 2, sc 1) in next 5 sts, sl st 6. Fasten off.

Pin the curved side of the wings to the sides of the body

# FRENCH HEN *(continued)*

(on top of the neck ruffles) with the feather details pointing toward the tail. With light purple yarn, sew just the front half of the wings to the body.

## COMB

With red yarn, ch 7.

Starting in 2nd ch from hook and working in back ridge loops, *(sl st 1, ch 5, sl st 1) in next st, sl st 1; rep from * 2 more times, ch 3 and sl st in current st. Fasten off.

With the ch-3 bump of comb in front, sew the comb down the top and back of the head.

## BEAK

With tan yarn, make a 4-st adjustable ring.

**Rnd 1:** Sc 4 and fasten off.

Sew open edge of beak to face. Weave in ends.

## WATTLE (MAKE 2)

With red, ch 6.

Sl st in back ridge loop of 3rd ch from hook and fasten off. Weave yarn tail through remaining 3 sts of ch and attach to top and left side of beak. Make a 2nd wattle and repeat on opposite side.

Glue or sew 4 mm plastic eyes or beads to the sides of the head. Using a single ply from your black yarn or black embroidery thread, apply 1 short stitch above each eye for an eyebrow.

## TAIL PLUME (MAKE 3)

With dark purple/light blue/green, make a 7-st adjustable ring. You will make one tail plume of each color.

**Rnd 1:** Sc 2 in next 3 sts, (hdc 1, dc 2, hdc 1) in next st, sc 2 in next 3 sts. (15 sts)

**Rnd 2:** Sl st 4, (sl st 1, ch 4, sl st 1) in next 2 sts, (sl st 1, ch 6, sl st 1) in next 3 sts, (sl st 1, ch 4, sl st 1) in next 2 sts, sl st 4.

Place the RS of the green tail plume against the WS of the blue tail plumes. Sew the sl st edges tog with a whip stitch. With WS of green facing up, sew the whipped stitch edge to the back of the body at the end of the back seam.

With WS facing up, place the dark purple tail plume over the blue and green plumes, offsetting the placement slightly closer to the middle of the back to cover the attachment point of the blue/green plumes. Sew the purple plume's sl st edge down.

Sew on a jump ring. Add a hanger (page 18).

# CALLING BIRD

······· DIFFICULTY: INTERMEDIATE * FINISHED SIZE: 2" TALL, 2 1/2" WIDE (5 X 6 CM) ·······

## ⇌ MATERIALS ⇌

- Sock weight yarn in dark gray, ivory, light blue, and yellow
- Hook size C (2.75 mm)
- (1) 2 1/2" (6 cm) twig
- (2) 4 mm plastic safety eyes or beads
- Craft glue or needle and thread
- Polyester fiberfill
- Tapestry needle
- Scissors
- (1) 8–10 mm jump ring
- Place marker

## BODY AND HEAD

With yellow yarn, make an 8-st adjustable ring.

**Rnd 1:** Sc 2 in each st around. (16 sts)

**Rnd 2:** *Sc 1, Sc 2 in next st; rep from * 7 more times. (24 sts)

**Rnd 3:** Sc 24.

Cut yellow. Change to ivory.

**Rnds 4–5:** Sc 24.

**Rnd 6:** *Sc 4, sc2tog; rep from * 3 more times. (20 sts)

**Rnd 7:** Sc 20.

**Rnd 8:** *Sc 3, sc2tog; rep from * 3 more times. (16 sts)

**Rnd 9:** Sc2tog 2 times, sc 8, sc2tog 2 times. (12 sts)

**Rnd 10:** Sl st 2, sc 2 in next st 2 sts, sc 4, sc 2 in next 2 sts, sl st 2. (16 sts)

**Rnds 11–12:** Sc 16.

**Rnd 13:** *Sc 2, sc2tog; rep from * 3 more times. (12 sts)

Stuff body.

**Rnd 14:** Sc2tog 6 times. (6 sts)

Stuff head, close hole, and fasten off.

## BACK AND TAIL

With light blue, ch 6.

**Row 1:** Working in back ridge loops, sc 2 in 2nd ch from hook, sc 3, sc 5 in back ridge loop of next st. Rotate ch so front loops are facing up. Starting in next ch and working in front loops, sc 3, sc 2 in next st, ch 1, turn. (15 sts)

**Row 2:** Sk ch 1, sc 2 in next 2 sts, hdc 3, sc 2 in next st, sc 3, sc 2 in next st, hdc 3, sc 2 in next 2 sts, ch 1, turn. (21 sts)

**Row 3:** Sk ch 1, sc 2 in next st, hdc 4, sc 2, sl st 2, sc 1, (sc 1, hdc 1, sc 1) in next st, sc 1, sl st 2, sc 2, hdc 4, sc 2 in next st, ch 1, turn. (25 sts)

**Row 4:** Sk ch 1, sc 8, (sc 1, hdc 1, ch 2, sl st in back ridge loop of 2nd ch from hook, sc 1) in next st, sl st 2, sc 1, (sc 1, hdc 1, ch 2, sl st in back ridge loop of 2nd ch from hook, sc 1) in next st, sc 1, sl st 2, (sc 1, hdc 1, ch 2, sl st in back ridge loop of 2nd ch from hook, sc 1) in next st, sc 8. Do not turn.

## TAIL DETAIL

**Rnd 5:** Ch 3 and work across the gap to first st in row 4. Sc in first st (counts as 1 sc) and work 6 more sc across the raw edges of the work. Cont to work the tail in the rnd. (7 sts)

**Rnd 6:** Work 3 sc around the ch 3 (into the space), sc 7. (10 sts)

**Rnd 7:** *Sc 4, sc 2 in next st; rep from * 1 more time. (12 sts)

**Rnd 8:** *Sc 5, sc 2 in next st; rep from * 1 more time. (14 sts)

**Rnd 9:** *Sc 5, sc2tog; rep from * 1 more time. (12 sts)

**Rnd 10:** *Sc 4, sc2tog; rep from * 1 more time. (10 sts)

Fasten off yarn, flatten end of tail, and sew seam closed.

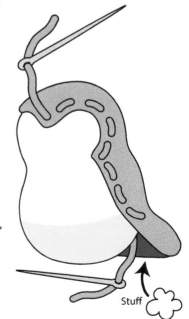

Stuff

# CALLING BIRD (continued)

## BEAK (MAKE 2)

With dark gray, make a 3-st adjustable ring. Pull yarn through last st to fasten off (do not join to first st in ring).

Stack the beak pieces and place the flat edges against the face directly under the light blue "peak" detail in the middle of the head. Sew beaks in place.

## CREST

With light blue, ch 10.

**Row 1:** Starting in 2nd ch from hook and working in back ridge loops, sl st 1, sc 2, hdc 1, dc 1, hdc 1, sc 2, sl st 1 and fasten off.

Fold crest in half to create a wedge shape and whip stitch the top edges tog. Attach the open edges along the base of the crest to the top of the head with the shorter end of the crest by the beak and the taller end of the crest at the back of the head.

Glue or sew 4 mm plastic eyes or beads to the front of the head on either side of the beak.

## WING (MAKE 2)

With light blue, make a 7-st adjustable ring.

**Rnd 1:** Sc 2 in next 3 sts, (hdc 1, dc 1, hdc 1) in next st, sc 2 in next 3 sts. (15 sts)

**Rnd 2:** Sc 2, sc 2 in next 2 sts, hdc 3, (hdc 1, dc 1, hdc 1) in next st, hdc 3, sc 2 in next 2 sts, sc 2. (21 sts)

### Left wing

**Rnd 3:** Sl st 6, (sc 1, ch 2, sc 1) in next 5 sts, sl st 10. Fasten off

### Right wing

**Rnd 3:** Sl st 10, (sc 1, ch 2, sc 1) in next 5 sts, sl st 6. Fasten off.

With RS facing you, hold one of the wings horizontally with the ruffle detail pointing down and fold the top third of the wing back. Tack the fold in place with a few light blue stitches. Repeat fold in the opposite side for the other wing (creating a mirror image). Sew the folded edge of the wings to the shoulders and upper back of the body.

With light blue yarn, add a few more stitches under the wing to hold the folded portion of the wing closer to the body.

## FEET

Cut (1) 2 1/2" (6 cm) twig. Double up dark gray yarn on a tapestry needle. Hold the left side of the stick against the lower belly of one bird and loop the yarn around the stick 3 to 4 times, catching the underside of the belly as you sew to create a foot. Repeat 1 more time to create the other foot.

Sew on a jump ring. Add a hanger (page 18).

# GOLDEN RINGS

······ DIFFICULTY: EASY * FINISHED SIZE: 3" TALL, 3" WIDE (8 X 8 CM) ······

## ⇟ MATERIALS ⇟

- Sock weight yarn in gold
- Hook size C (2.75 mm)
- (5) 1 1/8" (3 cm) plastic cabone rings
- 12" x 3/8" (31 cm x 10 mm) sheer ivory ribbon
- Tapestry needle
- Scissors
- (1) 8–10 mm jump ring
- Place marker

TO HiDe/secure THe yarn Tail aT THe Beg of your work, HOLD THe Tail againsT THe caBOne ring WHen working THe firsT 10 sc sTs anD THen Trim.

## RING (MAKE 5)

With gold, (sl st, ch 1, sc 1) around the edge of the 1 1/8" (3 cm) cabone ring (page 15) to attach yarn.

**Rnd 1:** Sc around the entire edge of the ring but do not join last st to first. Once ring is covered, twist the stitches around the ring until you have 5 spiral rotations. Sl st into first st on ring to join and fasten off.

Place the edges of 4 rings against each other to form a square shape and sew the connection points tog. Lay the 4 sewn-tog rings on a flat surface and place the 5th ring in the middle of the grouping of 4 and sew in place.

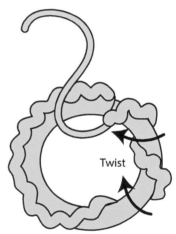

Twist

Attach jump ring to the side of one of the rings (page 18).

Tie the ribbon in a bow to the ring directly under the hanging loop. To secure the ribbon before tying a bow, apply the ribbon to the surface of the ring using a fringe knot technique. To keep ribbon ends from fraying, dab a light coating of craft glue to the undersides of the ribbon ends.

Sew on a jump ring. Add a hanger (page 18).

# GOOSE A-LAYING

······ DIFFICULTY: INTERMEDIATE * FINISHED SIZE: 3 1/2" TALL, 3" WIDE (9 X 8 CM) ······

## ⇟ MATERIALS ⇟

- Sock weight yarn in black, gold, dark gray, light gray, orange, tan, and white
- Hook size C (2.75 mm)
- (2) 4 mm plastic safety eyes
- Craft glue or needle and thread
- Polyester fiberfill
- Tapestry needle
- Scissors
- (1) 8–10 mm jump ring
- Place marker

## BODY

With white yarn, ch 5.

**Rnd 1:** Starting in 2nd ch from hook and working in back ridge loops, sc 3, sc 5 back ridge loop of next ch. Rotate ch so front loops are facing up. Starting in next ch and working in front loops, sc 2, sc 2 in fl of next ch. (12 sts)

**Rnd 2:** Sc 2 in next st, sc 2, hdc 2 in next 5 sts, sc 2, sc 2 in next 2 sts. (20 sts)

**Rnd 3:** Sc 2 in next 2 st, sc 4, hdc 2 in next 6 sts, sc 4, sc 2 in next 4 sts. (32 sts)

**Rnd 4:** Sc 32.

Cut white. Change to light gray.

**Rnds 5–9:** Sc 32.

### Start neck

**Rnd 10:** Sl st 9, sc 1, pm, sc 13.

Working across the rnd-10 sp, work first st of rnd 11 in the marked st of rnd 10.

**Rnd 11:** Sc 14.

**Rnd 12:** *Sc 5, sc2tog; rep from * 1 more time. (12 sts)

**Rnds 13–15:** Sc 12.

**Rnd 16:** *Sc 2, sc 2 in next st; rep from * 3 more times. (16 sts)

**Rnds 17–18:** Sc 16.

**Rnd 19:** *Sc 2, sc2tog; rep from * 3 more times. (12 sts)

**Rnd 20:** *Sc 1, sc2tog; rep from * 3 more times. (8 sts)

Fasten off yarn and stuff head and neck. Close hole at top of the head.

Stuff body and neck. Using light gray yarn, whip stitch seam closed along back of body.

## WING (MAKE 2)

With light gray yarn, make a 7-st adjustable ring.

**Rnd 1:** Sc 2 in next 3 sts, (hdc 1, dc 1, hdc 1) in next st, sc 2 in next 3 sts. (15 sts)

**Rnd 2:** Sc 2, sc 2 in next 2 sts, hdc 3, (hdc 1, dc 1, hdc 1) in next st, hdc 3, sc 2 in next 2 sts, sc 2. (21 sts)

Cut light gray. Change to dark gray.

### Left wing

**Rnd 3:** Sl st 6, (sc 1, ch 2, sc 1) in next 5 sts, sl st 10. Fasten off.

### Right wing

**Rnd 3:** Sl st 10, (sc 1, ch 2, sc 1) in next 5 sts, sl st 6. Fasten off.

Pin the curved side of the wings to the sides of the body with the ruffled feather detail pointing toward the tail. With dark gray, sew just the front half of the wings to the body. Weave in ends.

## TAIL FEATHERS

With light gray, ch 7.

Starting in 2nd ch from hook and working in back ridge loops, *(sl st 1, ch 5, sl st in at base of ch-5) in next st, sk 1; rep from * 2 more times.

# GOOSE A-LAYING (continued)

Fasten off, leaving a long yarn tail for sewing. Sew the first and last ch tog to form a ring. Sew ring to the back of goose body at the end of the back seam.

## BEAK

With orange, make a 3-st adjustable ring.

**Rnd 1:** Sc 1, sc 2 in next st, sc 1. (4 sts)

**Rnd 2:** Sc 1, hdc 2 in next 2 sts, sc 1. (6 sts)

**Rnd 3:** Sc 6.

Fasten off.

With the hdc sts from rnd 2 facing up, attach open edge of beak to the front of the head.

Glue or sew 4 mm plastic eyes or beads to the sides of the head. Using a single yarn ply from your black yarn or black embroidery thread, apply 1 short stitch above each eye for an eyebrow.

## FOOT (MAKE 2)

With orange, make a 7-st adjustable ring. Do not join. Ch 1, turn.

**Row 1:** Sk ch 1, sl st 3, *ch-3, sl st in st at base of ch-3, sl st 1; rep from * 2 more times, sl st 1.

Fasten off in skipped ch 1, leaving a long tail.

Attach feet to the front half of the underside of the body, leaving the toes loose.

## EGG

With gold, make a 6-st adjustable ring.

**Rnd 1:** Sc 2 in each st around. (12 sts)

**Rnd 2:** *Sc 1, sc 2 in next st; rep from * 5 more times. (18 sts)

**Rnds 3–4:** Sc 18.

**Rnd 5:** *Sc 7, sc2tog; rep from * 1 more time. (16 sts)

**Rnd 6:** *Sc 6, sc2tog; rep from * 1 more time. (14 sts)

**Rnd 7:** *Sc 5, sc2tog; rep from * 1 more time. (12 sts)

**Rnd 8:** *Sc 4, sc2tog; rep from * 1 more time. (10 sts)

**Rnd 9:** Sc 10.

**Rnd 10:** *Sc 3, sc2tog; rep from * 1 more time. (8 sts)

Stuff egg.

**Rnd 11:** *Sc 2, sc2tog; rep from * 1 more time. (6 sts)

Fasten off, close hole, and weave in ends.

Lay the egg on its side and place goose on top of egg. Using orange yarn, sew the feet and toes around the top half of the egg.

## NEST

Make a pom-pom of tan yarn by wrapping the yarn 30 times around 3 fingers and trimming the loops to create a bundle of yarn strands. Tie the bundle in the middle and trim to a diameter of about 1" to 1 1/2" (3 to 4 cm). Fluff the yarn with your fingers and sew to the bottom of the egg.

Sew on a jump ring. Add a hanger (page 18).

# SWAN A-SWIMMING

······ DIFFICULTY: INTERMEDIATE * FINISHED SIZE: 2 1/2˝ TALL, 3˝ WIDE (6 X 8 CM) ······

## ⇌ MATERIALS ⇌

- Sock weight yarn in black, orange, and white
- Hook size C (2.75 mm)
- (2) 4 mm plastic safety eyes
- Craft glue or needle and thread
- Polyester fiberfill
- Tapestry needle
- Scissors
- (1) 8–10 mm jump ring
- Place marker

## BODY

With white, ch 5.

**Rnd 1:** Starting in 2nd ch from hook and working in back ridge loops, sc 3, sc 5 in back ridge loop of next ch. Rotate ch so front loops are facing up. Starting in next ch and working in front loops, sc 2, sc 2 in fl of next ch. (12 sts)

**Rnd 2:** Sc 2 in next st, sc 2, hdc 2 in next 5 sts, sc 2, sc 2 in next 2 sts. (20 sts)

**Rnd 3:** Sc 2 in next st, sc 5, hdc 2 in next 6 sts, sc 5, sc 2 in next 3 sts. (30 sts)

**Rnds 4–8:** Sc 30.

### Start neck

**Rnd 9:** Sl st 8, sc 1, pm, sc 13.

Working across the rnd-9 sp, work first st of rnd 10 in the marked st of rnd 9.

**Rnd 10:** Sc 14.

**Rnd 11:** *Sc 5, sc2tog; rep from * 1 more time. (12 sts)

**Rnds 12–15:** Sc 12.

**Rnd 16:** *Sc 4, sc2tog; rep from * 1 more time. (10 sts)

**Rnds 17–19:** Sc 10.

**Rnd 20:** *Sc 3, sc2tog; rep from * 1 more time. (8 sts)

**Rnd 21:** *Sc 1, sc 2 in next st; rep from * 3 more times. (12 sts)

**Rnds 22–25:** Sc 12.

**Rnd 26:** *Sc 4, sc2tog; rep from * 1 more time. (10 sts)

**Rnd 27:** *Sc 3, sc2tog; rep from * 1 more time. (8 sts)

Fasten off yarn and stuff head and neck. Close hole at front of head.

Stuff body and neck. Using white, whip stitch seam closed along back of the body.

Fold head down toward neck and tack in place with a few stitches. Tilt neck back a bit and tack the base of the neck to the top of the back with a few stitches.

## WING (MAKE 2)

With white, make a 7-st adjustable ring.

**Rnd 1:** Sc 2 in next 3 sts, (hdc 1, dc 1, hdc 1) in next st, sc 2 in next 3 sts. (15 sts)

**Rnd 2:** Sc 2, sc 2 in next 2 sts, hdc 3, (hdc 1, dc 1, hdc 1) in next st, hdc 3, sc 2 in next 2 sts, sc 2. (21 sts)

**Rnd 3:** Sc 3, sc 2 in next 3 sts, hdc 4, (hdc 1, dc 1, hdc 1) in next st, hdc 4, sc 2 in next 3 sts, sc 3. (29 sts)

### Left wing

**Rnd 4:** Sl st 8, (sl st 1, ch 4, sl st 1) in next 4 sts, (sl st 1, ch 6, sl st 1) in next 5 sts, (sl st 1, ch 4, sl st 1) in next st, sl st 11.

### Right wing

**Rnd 4:** Sl st 11, (sl st 1, ch 4, sl st 1) in next st, (sl st 1, ch 6, sl st 1) in next 5 sts, (sl st 1, ch 4, sl st 1) in next 4 sts, sl st 8.

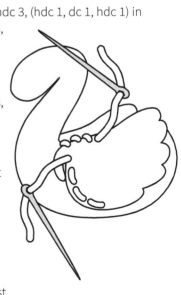

# SWAN A-SWIMMING (continued)

Holding wing horizontal with the ruffle detail pointing toward the back of the body, fold back the sl st 11 section of the wing edge and tack in place with a few stitches. Sew the front corner of the folded edge to the shoulder of the swan body. Sew the sl st 8 front edge of the wing to the body.

## TAIL FEATHERS (MAKE 2)

With white, make a 7-st adjustable ring.

**Rnd 1:** Sc 2 in next 3 sts, (hdc 1, dc 1, hdc 1) in next st, sc 2 in next 3 sts. (15 sts)

**Rnd 2:** Sl st 4, (sl st 1, ch 4, sl st 1) in next 2 sts, (sl st 1, ch 6, sl st 1) in next 3 sts, (sl st 1, ch 4, sl st 1) in next 2 sts, sl st 4.

Place the RS of one of the tail feathers against the back side of the swan body. Sew the bottom edge of the tail feathers to the back of the bird so the feathers curl up and toward the back of the swan. Repeat with the 2nd tail feather slightly lower on the backside of the swan to allow it to overlap the attachment point of the first tail feather.

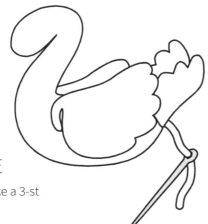

## BEAK AND FACE

With orange yarn, make a 3-st adjustable ring.

**Rnd 1:** Sc 1, sc 2 in next st, sc 1. (4 sts)

**Rnd 2:** Sc 4.

Cut orange. Change to black.

**Rnd 3:** In bl, sc 2 in each st around. (8 sts)

**Rnd 4:** Sc 2, ch 4, sk ch-4, sc 4, ch 4, sk ch-4, sc 2.

Fasten off.

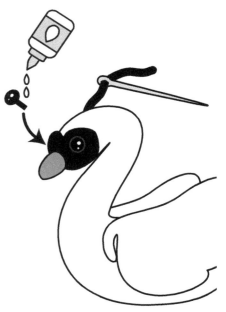

Stretch face around front of head and pin in place. There will be two eye holes at the ch-4 sps of rnd 4. Sew in place with black yarn. Glue or sew 4-mm plastic eyes or beads to the sides of the face in the ch-4 sp eye holes.

Sew on a jump ring. Add a hanger (page 18).

# MAID A-MILKING

······ DIFFICULTY: INTERMEDIATE * FINISHED SIZE: 3 1/4" TALL, 1 1/2" WIDE (8 X 4 CM) ······

## ⇒ MATERIALS ⇐

- Sock weight yarn in blue, brown, light gray, light yellow, tan, and white
- Hook size C (2.75 mm)
- Tapestry needle
- White felt
- Craft glue or sewing needle and white thread
- Scissors
- Polyester fiberfill
- (1) 8–10 mm jump ring
- Place marker

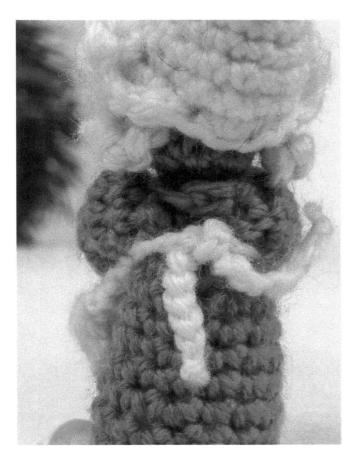

## HEAD AND BODY

With tan yarn, make a 6-st adjustable ring.

**Rnd 1:** Sc 2 in each st around. (12 sts)

**Rnd 2:** *Sc 2, sc 2 in next st; rep from * 3 more times. (16 sts)

**Rnds 3–5:** Sc 16.

**Rnd 6:** *Sc 2, sc2tog; rep from * 3 more times. (12 sts)

Stuff head.

**Rnd 7:** Sc2tog 6 times. (6 sts)

Cut tan. Change to blue.

**Rnd 8:** In bl, *sc 2, sc 2 in next st; rep from * 1 more time. (8 sts)

**Rnd 9:** *Sc 3, sc 2 in next st; rep from * 1 more time. (10 sts)

**Rnd 10:** *Sc 4, sc 2 in next st; rep from * 1 more time. (12 sts)

**Rnds 11–12:** Sc 12.

**Rnd 13:** *Sc 5, sc 2 in next st; rep from * 1 more time. (14 sts)

**Rnd 14:** Sc 14.

**Rnd 15:** *Sc 6, sc 2 in next st; rep from * 1 more time. (16 sts)

**Rnd 16:** Sc 16.

**Rnd 17:** *Sc 7, sc 2 in next st; rep from * 1 more time. (18 sts)

**Rnd 18:** BPsc 18.

Stuff body.

**Rnd 19:** *Sc 1, sc2tog; rep from * 5 more times. (12 sts)

**Rnd 20:** Sc2tog 6 times. (6 sts)

Fasten off, close hole, and weave in end.

## COLLAR DETAIL

**Rnd 1:** With head pointed up and working with blue yarn, (sl st 1, ch 1, sc 1) in one of the exposed front loops above rnd 8. Cont to work 5 more sc sts into the exposed front loops. (6 sts) Fasten off and weave in end.

# MAID A-MILKING *(continued)*

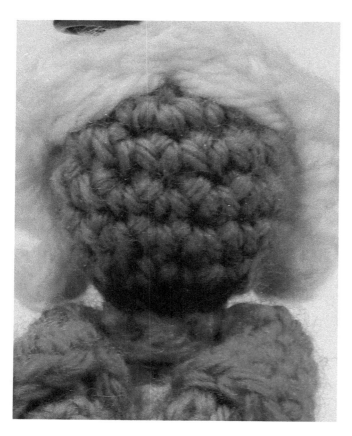

**Rnd 5:** Sc 2 in each st around. (8 sts)

**Rnd 6:** In bl, sc 8.

**Rnd 7:** Sc 8.

**Rnd 8:** *Sc 2, sc2tog; rep from * 1 more time. (6 sts)

Fasten off and stuff arm lightly. Close hole at top of shoulder.

## SLEEVE DETAIL

**Rnd 1:** With hand pointed up and working with blue yarn, (sl st 1, ch 1, sc 1) in one of the exposed front loops above rnd 6. Cont to work 7 more sc sts into the exposed front loops. (8 sts)

**Rnd 2:** Sc 8.

Fasten off and weave in end.

Sew the shoulders to the sides of the body on either side of the neck. Position the hands at the front of the body and sew the sides of the hands tog.

## SKIRT DETAIL

**Rnd 1:** With head pointing down and working with blue yarn, (sl st 1, ch 1, sc 2) in one of the exposed BPsc sts from rnd 18. Sc 1, *sc 2 in next st, sc 1; rep from * 8 more times in the remaining exposed BPsc sts of rnd 18. (27 sts) Fasten off and weave in end.

## HAND AND ARM (MAKE 2)

With tan yarn, make a 3-st adjustable ring.

**Rnd 1:** *Sc 2 in each st around. (6 sts)

**Rnd 2:** Sc 6.

**Rnd 3:** *Sc 1, sc2tog; rep from * 1 more time. (4 sts)

Cut tan. Change to blue.

**Rnd 4:** FPsc 4.

## APRON

With white, ch 5. Leave a 12" (31 cm) tail at the beg.

**Row 1:** Starting in 2nd ch from hook, sc 4, ch 1, turn. (4 sts)

**Row 2:** Sk ch 1, sc 4, ch 1, turn. (4 sts)

**Row 3:** Sk ch 1, sc 2 in next st, sc 2, sc 2 in next st, ch 1, turn. (6 sts)

**Rows 4–5:** Sk ch 1, sc 6, ch 1, turn. (6 sts)

**Row 6:** Sk ch 1, sc 2 in next st, sc 4, sc 2 in next st, ch 1, turn. (8 sts)

**Rows 7–9:** Sk ch 1, sc 8, ch 1, turn. (8 sts)

Sl st along the side edge of rows 9–1, sl st 4 across row 1, sl st side edge of rows 1–9. Fasten off.

## APRON TIES

Using the leftover yarn tail at the beg of the work, ch 15 and fasten off. Attach a 2nd piece of 12" (31 cm) white yarn to the opposite end of row 1, ch 15. Fasten off.

Tie the apron at the back of the body with a square knot.

## BONNET

With white, make a 3-st adjustable ring.

**Rnd 1:** Sc 3.

**Rnd 2:** Sc 2 in each st around. (6 sts)

**Rnd 3:** *Sc 2, sc 2 in next st; rep from * 1 more time. (8 sts)

**Rnd 4:** *Sc 3, sc 2 in next st; rep from * 1 more time. (10 sts)

**Rnd 5:** *Sc 4, sc 2 in next st; rep from * 1 more time. (12 sts)

**Rnd 6:** *Sc 2, sc 2 in next st; rep from * 3 more times. (16 sts)

**Rnd 7:** Sc 16.

**Rnd 8:** Sc 6, (sl st 1, sc 1) in next st, (hdc 1, dc 1, hdc 1) in next st, (sc 1, sl st 1) in next st, sc 4, (sl st 1, sc 1) in next st, (hdc 1, dc 1, hdc 1) in next st, (sc 1, sl st 1) in next st. (24 sts)

**Rnd 9:** Sc2tog 3 times, sl st 2, sc 1, (hdc 1, ch 2, sl st in back ridge loop of 2nd ch from hook, hdc 1) in next st, sc 1, sl st 2, FPsc 4, sl st 2, sc 1, (hdc 1, ch 2, sl st in back ridge loop of 2nd ch from hook, hdc 1) in next st, sc 1, sl st 2. Fasten off.

Stuff bonnet lightly.

With the rnd 9 FPsc 4 sts positioned in the front, place top and back of head into bonnet and sew in place.

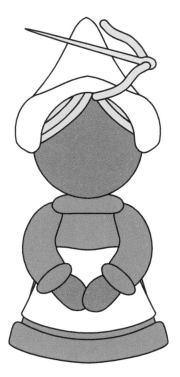

## HAIR DETAIL

With light yellow, apply a grouping of 3 to 4 long stitches from the top of the forehead to the left side of the head (working just under the edge of the bonnet). Allow stitches to hang loosely and repeat the process working to the right side of the head.

## BRAID (MAKE 2)

With light yellow, loosely ch 5 while holding both the working yarn and the yarn tail tog as you ch (to double up the yarn). Trim loose ends short. Attach rounded end of the braid to the side of the head under the bonnet. Repeat for the other side of the head.

## MILK PAIL

With light gray, make a 4-st adjustable ring.

**Rnd 1:** Sc 2 in each st around. (8 sts)

**Rnd 2:** BPsc 8.

**Rnd 3:** *Sc 3, sc 2 in next st; rep from * 1 more time. (10 sts)

**Rnd 4:** Sc 10.

**Rnd 5:** *Sc 4, sc 2 in next st; rep from * 1 more time. (12 sts)

**Rnd 6:** FPsc 12.

Lightly stuff pail. Cut (1) 1/2" (13 mm) circle from white felt and glue over opening at the top of the pail. With brown yarn and a tapestry needle, draw the yarn through one side of the pail, through the sides of the hands, and to the opposite side of the pail for a handle. Fasten off.

Sew on a jump ring. Add a hanger (page 18).

# LADY DANCING

······ DIFFICULTY: INTERMEDIATE * FINISHED SIZE: 3 3/4˝ TALL, 2 1/4˝ WIDE (10 X 6 CM) ······

## ⇻ MATERIALS ⇺

- Sock weight yarn in brown, dark green, ivory, magenta, tan, and white
- Hook size C (2.75 mm)
- (2) 4 mm white beads
- Invisible thread
- Beading needle
- Tapestry needle
- Large pin
- Scissors
- Polyester fiberfill
- (1) 8–10 mm jump ring
- Place marker

## HEAD AND BODY

With tan yarn, make a 6-st adjustable ring.

**Rnd 1:** Sc 2 in each st around. (12 sts)

**Rnd 2:** *Sc 2, sc 2 in next st; rep from * 3 more times. (16 sts)

**Rnds 3–5:** Sc 16.

**Rnd 6:** *Sc 2, sc2tog; rep from * 3 more times. (12 sts)

Stuff head.

**Rnd 7:** Sc2tog 6 times. (6 sts)

Cut tan. Change to dark green.

**Rnd 8:** In bl, *sc 2, sc 2 in next st; rep from * 1 more time. (8 sts)

**Rnd 9:** *Sc 3, sc 2 in next st; rep from * 1 more time. (10 sts)

**Rnd 10:** *Sc 4, sc 2 in next st; rep from * 1 more time. (12 sts)

**Rnd 11:** Sc 12.

Cut dark green. Change to ivory.

**Rnd 12:** In bl, sc 12.

**Rnd 13:** *Sc 5, sc 2 in next st; rep from * 1 more time. (14 sts)

**Rnd 14:** Sc 14.

**Rnd 15:** *Sc 6, sc 2 in next st; rep from * 1 more time. (16 sts)

**Rnd 16:** *Sc 7, sc 2 in next st; rep from * 1 more time. (18 sts)

**Rnd 17:** BPsc 18.

Stuff body.

**Rnd 18:** Sc2tog 9 times. (9 sts)

Fasten off, stuff body, close hole, and weave in ends.

## COLLAR DETAIL

**Rnd 1:** With head pointed up and working with dark green yarn, (sl st 1, ch 1, sc 1) in one of the exposed fl above rnd 8. Cont to work 5 more sc sts into the exposed fl. (6 sts)

Fasten off and weave in end.

# LADY DANCING (continued)

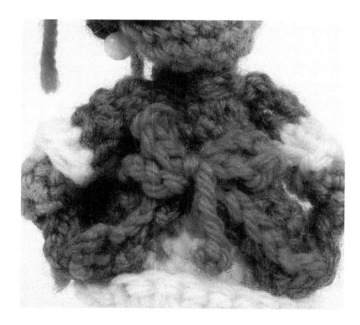

## SKIRT DETAIL

**Rnd 1:** With head pointing down and working with ivory yarn, (sl st 1, ch 1, sc 2) in one exposed BPsc st from rnd 17. Sc 1, *sc 2 in next st, sc 1; rep from * 7 more times in the remaining exposed BPsc sts of rnd 17. (27 sts)

**Rnd 2:** Sc 27.

Fasten off and weave in end.

## OUTER SKIRT

With dark green yarn, ch 13.

**Row 1:** Starting in 2nd ch from hook, sc 12, ch 1, turn. (12 sts)

**Row 2:** Sk ch 1, sc 3, sc 2 in next st, sc 4, sc 2 in next st, sc 3, ch 1, turn. (14 sts)

**Row 3:** Sk ch 1, sc2tog, *sc 2 in next st, sc 1; rep from * 1 more time, sc 2, **sc 1, sc 2 in next st; rep from ** 1 more time, sc2tog, ch 1, turn. (16 sts)

**Row 4:** Sk ch 1, sc 4, *sc 2 in next st, sc 1; rep from * 1 more time, **sc 1, sc 2 in next st; rep from ** 1 more time, sc 4, ch 1, turn. (20 sts)

**Row 5:** Sk ch 1, sc2tog, *sc 2 in next st, sc 3; rep from * 1 more time, **sc 3, sc 2 in next st; rep from ** 1 more time, sc2tog, ch 1, turn. (22 sts)

**Row 6:** Sk ch 1, sc2tog, sc 2 in next 18, sc2tog. (38 sts)

Change to magenta and sl st around the entire perimeter of piece. Fasten off.

Attach row 1 of outer skirt around rnd 11 of body. The opening of the skirt will be in the front.

## BOW DETAIL

With magenta, ch 26. Carefully insert a pin through the body from back to front so the sharp point is sticking out where the outer skirt comes tog in the front. Place the center of the ch-26 onto the point of the pin. Shape two loops on each half and use the pin end to hold the bow shaping in place. Using magenta yarn and the tapestry needle, apply 2 to 3 short stitches over the center of the bow to hold the shaping in place. Remove the pin and trim the yarn tails at the ends of the ch-26 short.

## LEG (MAKE 2)

With brown yarn, make a 3-st adjustable ring.

**Rnd 1:** Sc 2 in each st around. (6 sts)

**Rnd 2:** Sc 6.

Cut brown. Change to white.

**Rnds 3–4:** Sc 6.

Fasten off. Stuff leg lightly. Attach open edges of legs to the hips of the body under the dress.

## HAND AND ARM (MAKE 2)

With tan yarn, make a 3-st adjustable ring.

**Rnd 1:** Sc 2 in each st around. (6 sts)

**Rnd 2:** *Sc 1, sc2tog; rep from * 1 more time. (4 sts)

Stuff hand.

Cut tan. Change to ivory.

**Rnd 3:** FPsc 4.

**Rnd 4:** In bl, *sc 1, sc 2 in next st, rep from * 1 more time. (6 sts)

Cut ivory. Change to green.

**Rnd 5:** FPsc 6.

**Rnd 6:** *Sc 2, sc 2 in next st; rep from * 1 more time. (8 sts)

**Rnd 7:** *Sc 2, sc2tog; rep from * 1 more time. (6 sts)

Fasten off and stuff arm lightly. Close hole at top of arm.

## SLEEVE DETAIL

**Rnd 1:** With hand pointed up and using white yarn, (sl st 1, ch 1, sc 1) in one of the exposed fl above rnd 4. Cont to work sc 2 in next st, sc 1, sc 2 in next st into the exposed fl. (6 sts)

Fasten off and weave in ends.

Sew the shoulders to the sides of the body on either side of the neck. With dark green, sew the hands to the hem of the dress.

## HAIR

With brown, make a 6-st adjustable ring.

**Rnd 1:** Sc 2 in each st around. (12 sts)

**Rnd 2:** Sc2tog 6 times. (6 sts)

**Rnd 3:** *Sc 2, sc 2 in next st; rep from * 1 more time. (8 sts)

Stuff bun lightly.

**Rnd 4:** Sc 2 in each st around. (16 sts)

**Rnd 5:** *Sc 3, sc 2 in next st; rep from * 3 more times. (20 sts)

**Rnd 6:** (Sl st 1, hdc 2) in next st, (hdc 1, sc 1) in next st, sl st 1, (sc 1, hdc 1) in next st, (hdc 2, sl st 1) in next st, sk 1, sl st 1, sk 1, sl st 1, sc 7, sk 1, sl st 1, sk 1, sl st 1. (22 sts)

**Rnd 7:** Sl st 1, sc 4, sl st 1, sc 4, sl st 1, sk 1, sl st 1, sk 1, sl st 1, sc 2 in next st, sl st 2, sc 2 in next st, sk 1, sl st 1, sk 1, sl st 1. (21 sts)

Place the hair on the head and sew the edge down with small running stitches.

## HAIR BAND

Double up green and magenta yarn. Ch 8 while holding the strands tog. Wrap hair band around base of hair bun and secure in back. Trim the yarn tails to 2" (5 cm) long and let hang.

Sew a 4 mm white bead to the sides of the head for earrings with a beading needle and invisible thread.

Sew on a jump ring. Add a hanger (page 18).

# LORD A-LEAPING

······ DIFFICULTY: INTERMEDIATE * FINISHED SIZE: 3" TALL, 2 1/2" WIDE (8 X 6 CM) ······

## ⇌ MATERIALS ⇌

- Sock weight yarn in black, brown, dark purple, lavender, tan, and white
- Hook size C (2.75 mm)
- Tapestry needle
- Felt in black and gold/yellow
- Scissors
- (1) 6 mm gold metallic bead
- Beading needle
- Invisible thread
- Polyester fiberfill
- Craft glue or needle and thread
- (1) 8–10 mm jump ring
- Place marker

## HEAD AND BODY

With tan yarn, make a 6-st adjustable ring.

**Rnd 1:** Sc 2 in each st around. (12 sts)

**Rnd 2:** *Sc 2, sc 2 in next st; rep from * 3 more times. (16 sts)

**Rnds 3–5:** Sc 16.

**Rnd 6:** *Sc 2, sc2tog; rep from * 3 more times. (12 sts)

Stuff head.

**Rnd 7:** Sc2tog 6 times. (6 sts)

Cut tan. Change to dark purple.

**Rnd 8:** In bl, *sc 2, sc 2 in next st; rep from * 1 more time. (8 sts)

**Rnd 9:** Sc 2 in each st around. (16 sts)

**Rnd 10:** BPsc 16. (16 sts)

**Rnds 11–13:** Sc 16.

**Rnd 14:** BPsc 16.

Stuff body.

**Rnd 15:** Sc2tog 8 times. (8 sts)

Fasten off, close hole, and weave in end.

## COLLAR DETAIL

**Rnd 1:** With head pointed up and working with dark purple yarn, (sl st 1, ch 1, sc 1) in one of the exposed fl above rnd 8. Cont to work 5 more sc sts into the exposed fl. (6 sts)

Fasten off and weave in end.

## JACKET DETAIL

**Rnd 1:** With head pointed down and working with dark purple yarn, (sl st 1, ch 1, sc 1) at the back of the body in one of the rnd 14 exposed BPsc sts. Cont to work 15 more sc sts into the exposed BPsc sts of rnd 14. (16 sts)

Cut dark purple. Change to lavender.

**Rnd 2:** Sl st in each st around. (16 sts)

Fasten off and weave in end.

# LORD A-LEAPING *(continued)*

## HAND AND ARM (MAKE 2)

With tan yarn, make a 3-st adjustable ring.

**Rnd 1:** Sc 2 in each st around. (6 sts)

**Rnds 2–3:** Sc 6.

Cut tan. Change to white.

**Rnd 4:** FPsc 6.

**Rnd 5:** In bl, sc 6.

**Rnd 6:** Sc 6.

Cut white. Change to dark purple.

**Rnd 7:** FPsc 6.

**Rnd 8:** In bl, sc 6.

Fasten off. Weave yarn tail through bl of rnd 8 and pull to close. The fl should still be visible.

## SLEEVE DETAIL

**Rnd 1:** With hand pointed up and working with white yarn, (sl st 1, ch 1, sc 1) in one of the rnd 5 exposed front loops.

Cont to work 5 more sc sts into the exposed front loops. (6 sts)

Fasten off and weave in end.

## SHOULDER SLEEVE DETAIL

**Rnd 1:** With hand pointed up and working with lavender yarn, (sl st 1, ch 1, sc 1) in one of the rnd 8 exposed front loops. Cont to work 5 more sc sts into the exposed front loops. (6 sts)

Fasten off and weave in end. Push shoulder cap down to cover upper arm.

Sew side of shoulder sleeves to the shoulders of the body. Leave arms loose.

## LEG (MAKE 2)

With brown yarn, make a 3-st adjustable ring.

**Rnd 1:** Sc 2 in each st around. (6 sts)

**Rnd 2:** Sc 6.

Cut brown. Change to white.

**Rnds 3–6:** Sc 6.

Fasten off. Stuff leg lightly.

Attach open edges of legs to the bottom of the body. Position the legs into a leaping pose. Secure in place with a few stitches.

## HAT

With lavender yarn, make a 6-st adjustable ring and leave a 12" (30 cm) yarn tail at beg of work.

**Rnd 1:** Sc 2 in each st around. (12 sts)

**Rnd 2:** *Sc 1, sc 2 in next st; rep from * 5 more times. (18 sts)

**Rnd 3:** *Sc 2, sc 2 in next st; rep from * 5 more times. (24 sts)

**Rnd 4:** *Sc 4, sc2tog; rep from * 3 more times. (20 sts)

**Rnd 5:** *Sc 3, sc2tog; rep from * 3 more times. (16 sts)

**Rnd 6:** Sc 16.

Cut lavender. Change to black.

**Rnd 7:** FPsc 4, in fl; sl st 1, sc 1, hdc 2 in next 2 sts, sc 1, sl st 1. Tbl, FPsc 4.

Fasten off.

Place a small amount of stuffing into the hat and pull the hat halfway down onto the head with the brim detail from rnd 7 at the front. Sew the edge of the hat to the head. Thread the leftover yarn tail at beg of work back and forth through the top of the hat and the top of the head, pulling gently to sink the top of the hat. Fasten off yarn at the base of the hat in the back.

With a beading needle and invisible thread, sew a 6 mm gold metallic bead to the top of the hat.

## BELT

With black felt, cut out (1) 1/4" x 3 1/4" (6 mm x 8 cm) strip. Wrap felt around jacket for a belt, trim to fit, and secure the ends in the back. With gold/yellow felt, cut out (1) 1/4" x 3/8" (6 x 10 mm) rectangle. Attach felt rectangle to the front of the belt for a buckle.

Sew on a jump ring. Add a hanger (page 18).

# PIPER PIPING

DIFFICULTY: INTERMEDIATE * FINISHED SIZE: 3" TALL, 1 1/4" WIDE (8 X 3 CM)

## ⇌ MATERIALS ⇌

- Sock weight yarn in black, blue, brown, gold, ivory, tan, and white
- Hook size C (2.75 mm)
- Tapestry needle
- Felt in black and gold/yellow
- (6–8) 11/0 silver seed beads
- 3" (8 cm) 16-gauge copper or bronze wire
- Round-nose flat pliers
- Scissors
- Beading needle
- Invisible thread
- Polyester fiberfill
- Craft glue or needle and thread
- (1) 8–10 mm jump ring
- Place marker

## HEAD AND BODY

With tan yarn, make a 6-st adjustable ring.

**Rnd 1:** Sc 2 in each st around. (12 sts)

**Rnd 2:** *Sc 2, sc 2 in next st; rep from * 3 more times. (16 sts)

**Rnds 3–5:** Sc 16.

**Rnd 6:** *Sc 2, sc2tog; rep from * 3 more times. (12 sts)

Stuff head.

**Rnd 7:** Sc2tog 6 times. (6 sts)

Cut tan. Change to blue.

**Rnd 8:** In bl, *sc 2, sc 2 in next st; rep from * 1 more time. (8 sts)

**Rnd 9:** Sc 2 in each st around. (16 sts)

**Rnds 10–13:** Sc 16.

**Rnd 14:** BPsc 16.

Stuff body.

**Rnd 15:** Sc2tog 8 times. (8 sts)

Fasten off, close hole, and weave in end.

## COLLAR DETAIL

**Rnd 1:** With head pointed up and using blue yarn, (sl st 1, ch 1, sc 1) in one of the exposed front loops above rnd 8. Cont to work 5 more sc sts into the exposed front loops. (6 sts)

Fasten off and weave in end.

## JACKET DETAIL

**Rnd 1:** With head pointed down and using gold yarn, (sl st 1, ch 1, sc 1) at the back of the body in one of the rnd 14 exposed loops. Cont to work 15 more sc sts into the exposed loops of rnd 13. (16 sts)

Cut gold. Change to blue.

**Rnd 2:** Sc in each st around.

Fasten off and weave in end.

# PIPER PIPING (continued)

## HAND AND ARM (MAKE 2)

With tan yarn, make a 3-st adjustable ring.

**Rnd 1:** Sc 2 in each st around. (6 sts)

**Rnd 2:** Sc 6.

**Rnd 3:** *Sc 1, sc2tog; rep from * 1 more time. (4 sts)

Cut tan. Change to blue.

**Rnd 4:** FPsc 4.

**Rnd 5:** Sc 2 in each st around. (8 sts)

**Rnd 6:** In bl, sc 8.

**Rnd 7:** Sc 8.

**Rnd 8:** *Sc 2, sc2tog; rep from * 1 more time. (6 sts)

Fasten off and stuff arm lightly. Close hole at top of shoulder.

## SLEEVE DETAIL

**Rnd 1:** With hand pointed up and using gold yarn, (sl st 1, ch 1, sc 1) in one of the exposed fl above rnd 6. Cont to work 7 more sc sts into the exposed fl. (8 sts)

Cut gold. Change to blue.

**Rnd 2:** Sc 8.

Fasten off and weave in end.

Sew tops of arms to the shoulders of the body.

## LEG (MAKE 2)

With black yarn, make a 6-st adjustable ring.

**Rnd 1:** In bl, sc 2, ch 3, sk ch 3, sk 3, sc 1. (6 sts)

**Rnd 2:** Sc 2, sc in each ch of ch-3, sc 1. (6 sts)

**Rnd 3:** Sc 6.

Cut black. Change to white.

**Rnd 4:** In bl, sc 6.

**Rnd 5:** Sc 6.

Fasten off, leaving a long tail for sewing.

## BOOT TOE DETAIL

**Rnd 1:** With black and starting in lower right corner of boot opening, reattach black yarn (sl st, ch 1, sc 1) to rejoin yarn (counts as first sc). Cont to sc in the remaining 5 sts around the inside of the boot opening. (6 sts)

**Rnd 2:** Sc 6.

Fasten off, leaving a long tail. Lightly stuff boot and leg and close hole. Use leftover yarn tail to patch any holes in the sides of the boot.

## BOOT CUFF DETAIL

**Rnd 1:** With boot pointed down and using black yarn, (sl st 1, ch 1, sc 1) in one of the rnd 4 exposed fl. Cont to work 5 more sc sts into the exposed fl of rnd 4. (6 sts)

Fasten off and weave in end. Fold boot cuff down.

Attach open edges of legs to the bottom of the body.

## HAIR

With brown, make an 8-st adjustable ring.

**Rnd 1:** Sc 2 in each st around. (16 sts)

**Rnd 2:** *Sc 3, sc 2 in next st; rep from * 3 more times. (20 sts)

**Rnd 3:** (Sl st 1, hdc 2) in next st, (hdc 1, sc 1) in next st, sl st 1, (sc 1, hdc 1) in next st, (hdc 2, sl st 1) in next st, sk 1, sl st 1, sk 1, sl st 1, sc 7, sk 1, sl st 1, sk 1, sl st 1. (22 sts)

**Rnd 4:** Sl st 1, sc 4, sl st 1, sc 4, sl st 1, sk 1, sl st 1, sk 1, sl st 1, sc 2 in next st, sl st 2, sc 2 in next st, sk 1, sl st 1, sk 1, sl st 1. (21 sts)

Place the hair on the head and sew the edge down with small running stitches.

## JACKET BACK FLAP

With blue, make a 4-st adjustable ring.

**Rnd 1:** Sc 3 in each st around. (12 sts)

**Rnd 2:** *Sc 1, sc 3 in next st, sc 1; rep from * 3 more times. (20 sts)

**Rnd 3:** Sl st 3, change to gold, sl st 15, change to blue, sl st 2.

Fasten off.

Sew blue edge of flap to back of shoulders.

## PIPE

With brown yarn, make a 4-st adjustable ring.

**Rnd 1:** In bl, sc 4.

**Rnds 2–7:** Sc 4.

**Rnd 8:** FPsc 4.

**Rnd 9:** Sc 2 in each st around. (8 sts)

Cut brown. Change to ivory.

**Rnd 10:** Sl st 8.

Fasten off.

Shape a mouthpiece with wire to match the illustration. Coat bottom half of mouthpiece with craft glue and insert into pipe. With invisible thread and beading needle, attach 6 to 8 silver seed beads to pipe for keys. Use tan yarn to attach finished pipe to hands. Put a small amount of glue onto end of mouthpiece and insert into front of head.

Sew on a jump ring. Add a hanger (page 18).

# DRUMMER DRUMMING

······ DIFFICULTY: INTERMEDIATE * FINISHED SIZE: 3 1/4" TALL, 1 1/2" WIDE (8 X 4 CM) ······

## ⚜ MATERIALS ⚜

- Sock weight yarn in black, gold, green, light gray, red, tan, and white
- Hook size C (2.75 mm)
- Tapestry needle
- White felt
- (14 to 16) 11/0 silver seed beads
- (1) 6/0 "E" red seed bead
- Invisible thread
- Beading needle
- (2) Ball head pins with plastic or glass heads
- Wire cutters
- Scissors
- Polyester fiberfill
- Craft glue or needle and thread
- (1) 8–10 mm jump ring
- Place marker

## HEAD AND BODY

With tan yarn, make a 6-st adjustable ring.

**Rnd 1:** Sc 2 in each st around. (12 sts)

**Rnd 2:** *Sc 2, sc 2 in next st; rep from * 3 more times. (16 sts)

**Rnds 3–5:** Sc 16.

**Rnd 6:** *Sc 2, sc2tog; rep from * 3 more times. (12 sts)

Stuff head.

**Rnd 7:** Sc2tog 6 times. (6 sts)

Cut tan. Change to green.

**Rnd 8:** In bl, *sc 2, sc 2 in next st; rep from * 1 more time. (8 sts)

**Rnd 9:** Sc 2 in each st around. (16 sts)

**Rnd 10:** BPsc 16.

**Rnds 11–13:** Sc 16.

**Rnd 14:** BPsc 16.

Stuff body.

**Rnd 15:** Sc2tog 8 times. (8 sts)

Fasten off, close hole, and weave in end.

## COLLAR DETAIL

**Rnd 1:** With head pointed up and using green yarn, (sl st 1, ch 1, sc 1) in one of the exposed fl above rnd 8. Cont to work 5 more sc sts into the exposed fl. (6 sts)

Fasten off and weave in end.

## JACKET DETAIL

**Rnd 1:** With head pointed down and using green yarn, (sl st 1, ch 1, sc 1) at the back of the body in one of the rnd 14 exposed loops. Cont to work 15 more sc sts into the exposed loops of rnd 14. (16 sts)

Fasten off and weave in end.

# DRUMMER DRUMMING (continued)

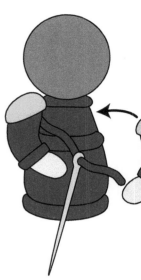

## HAND AND ARM (MAKE 2)

With white yarn, make a 3-st adjustable ring.

**Rnd 1:** Sc 2 in each st around. (6 sts)

**Rnds 2–3:** Sc 6.

Stuff hand.

Cut white. Change to green.

**Rnd 4:** FPsc 6.

**Rnd 5:** In bl, sc 6.

**Rnds 6–7:** Sc 6.

Cut green. Change to gold.

**Rnd 8:** FPsc 6.

Fasten off. Weave yarn tail through just the back loops of rnd 8, leaving the front loops exposed and pull to close.

## SLEEVE DETAIL

**Rnd 1:** With hand pointed up and using green yarn, (sl st 1, ch 1, sc 1) in one of the rnd 5 exposed front loops. Cont to work 5 more sc sts into the exposed front loops. (6 sts)

Fasten off and weave in end.

## SHOULDER CAP DETAIL

**Rnd 1:** With hand pointed up and using gold yarn, (sl st 1, ch 1, sc 1) in one of the rnd 8 exposed fl. Cont to work 5 more sc sts into the exposed fl. (6 sts)

Fasten off and weave in end. Push shoulder cap down to cover upper arm.

Sew side of shoulder caps to the shoulders of the body. With green yarn, tack the inside surfaces of the arms to the body to keep them from splaying out.

## LEG (MAKE 2)

With black yarn, make a 6-st adjustable ring.

**Rnd 1:** In bl, sc 2, ch 3, sk ch 3, sk 3, sc 1. (6 sts)

**Rnd 2:** Sc 2, sc in each ch of ch-3, sc 1. (6 sts)

**Rnd 3:** Sc 6.

Cut black. Change to white.

**Rnd 4:** In bl, sc 6.

**Rnd 5:** Sc 6.

Fasten off, leaving a long tail for sewing.

## BOOT TOE DETAIL

**Rnd 1:** With black and starting in lower right corner of boot opening, reattach black yarn (sl st, ch 1, sc 1) to rejoin yarn (counts as first sc). Cont to sc in the remaining 5 sts around the inside of the boot opening. (6 sts)

**Rnd 2:** Sc 6.

Fasten off, leaving a long tail. Lightly stuff boot and leg and close hole. Use leftover yarn tail to patch any holes in the sides of the boot.

## BOOT CUFF DETAIL

**Rnd 1:** With boot pointed down and using black yarn, (sl st 1, ch 1, sc 1) in one of the rnd 4 exposed fl. Cont to work 5 more sc sts into the exposed fl. (6 sts)

Fasten off and weave in end. Fold boot cuff down.

Attach open edges of legs to the bottom of the body.

## HAT

With green yarn, make a 6-st adjustable ring.

**Rnd 1:** Sc 2 in each st around. (12 sts)

**Rnd 2:** *Sc 1, sc 2 in next st; rep from * 5 more times. (18 sts)

**Rnd 3:** BPsc 18.

**Rnd 4:** Sc 18.

**Rnd 5:** *Sc 7, sc2tog; rep from * 1 more time. (16 sts)

**Rnds 6–7:** Sc 16.

Cut green. Change to black.

**Rnd 8:** FPsc 16.

**Rnd 9:** Sl st 5, in fl, sl st 1, sc 1, hdc 2 in next 2 sts, sc 1, sl st 1; tbl, sl st 5.

Fasten off. Lightly stuff hat.

Push upper half of head into the hat. Sew rnd 8 of the hat to the head. With green yarn and a tapestry needle, run yarn from the base of the neck, up through the head and top of the hat and back down again, pulling gently to flatten the top of the hat. Fasten off and weave in end.

With gold yarn, embroider 3 lazy daisy stitches to the front of the hat above the brim. Sew 1 red 6/0 "E" bead to the base of the embroidered design.

## DRUM

With red, make an 8-st adjustable ring.

**Rnd 1:** Sc 2 in each st around. (16 sts)

**Rnd 2:** BPsc 16.

**Rnds 3–5:** Sc 16.

**Rnd 6:** BPsc 16.

**Rnd 7:** Sc2tog 8 times. (8 sts)

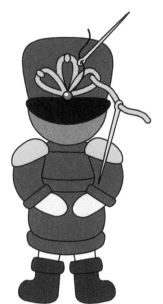

Stuff drum and close hole.

Run the yarn tail back and forth between the top and bottom of the drum and gently pull to flatten the surfaces. Weave in ends.

## DRUM RIM DETAIL

With the exposed loops of rnd 2 facing up, sl st in light gray into the exposed fl of rnd 2 and fasten off. Turn drum over and repeat on rnd 6 exposed fl.

## FURTHER DRUM DETAIL

With white, embroider long slanted lines along the sides of the drum (offset every 3 sts). With invisible thread and a beading needle, sew silver seed beads to the places where the lines come to a point.

Cut (1) 3/4" (19 mm) circle out of white felt and glue/sew it to the top of the drum.

Sew the side of the drum to the waist of the body. Position the arms so the hands rest above the drum and tack in place with a few stitches between the sleeves and the chest.

With wire cutters, trim the points off two ball head pins so they are 1" (3 cm) in length. Dab glue onto the trimmed pins and insert into the hands for drumsticks.

Sew on a jump ring. Add a hanger (page 18).

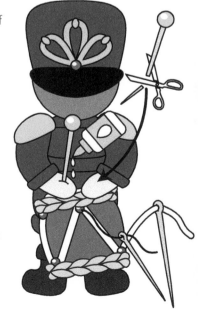

# WINTER FLORA

*T*his delightful collection of winter plants features all the holiday favorites, including holly, mistletoe, and my personal favorite—the traditional Christmas pickle! These ornaments work up quickly and look lovely attached to gift boxes or tied to a bottle of wine.

# PINECONE

······· DIFFICULTY: EASY \* FINISHED SIZE: 2 1/4" TALL, 1 3/4" WIDE (6 X 4 CM) ·······

## ⇌ MATERIALS ⇌

- Sock weight yarn in brown
- Hook size C (2.75 mm)
- Polyester fiberfill
- Tapestry needle
- White puffy fabric paint
- Glitter in coarse and fine white
- Long pointy stick (e.g., knitting needle, thin paint brush handle, chopstick)
- Scissors
- (1) 8–10 mm jump ring
- Place marker

## PINECONE

With brown, make an 8-st adjustable ring.

**Work rnds 1–9 in bl only.**

**Rnd 1:** Hdc 2 in each st around. (16 sts)

**Rnd 2:** Hdc 1, hdc 2 in next st, \*hdc 2, hdc 2 in next st, hdc 1; rep from \* 2 more times, hdc 2 in next st, hdc 1. (21 sts)

**Rnds 3–4:** Hdc 21.

**Rnd 5:** Hdc 1, \*hdc 4, sk 1, hdc 1; rep from \* 2 more times, hdc 2. (18 sts)

**Rnd 6:** Hdc 18.

**Rnd 7:** \*Sc 4, sc2tog; rep from \* 2 more times. (15 sts)

**Rnd 8:** \*Sc 1, sc2tog; rep from \* 4 more times. (10 sts)

Stuff pinecone.

**Rnd 9:** Sc2tog 5 times. (5 sts)

## PINECONE SCALE DETAIL

Ch 1, turn.

Working in the exposed front loops on the surface of the pinecone, \*sl st 1, (sl st 1, sc 1, hdc 1) in next st, (hdc 1, sc 1, sl st 1) in next st, sl st 1; rep from \* around to the top of the pinecone.

## SNOW

Place pinecone onto knitting needle, paintbrush handle, or chopstick to make "snow" application easier. Apply white fabric paint to edges of pinecone scales. If desired, dust the wet fabric paint with coarse white glitter followed immediately with fine white glitter. Put pinecone aside to dry completely. Once dry, shake off excess glitter by rolling pinecone between your hands.

Sew on a jump ring. Add a hanger (page 18).

# HOLLY

······ DIFFICULTY: EASY * FINISHED LEAF SIZE: 2" TALL, 1" WIDE (5 X 3 CM) ······

## ⚜ MATERIALS ⚜

- Sock weight yarn in dark green and red
- Hook size C (2.75 mm)
- Polyester fiberfill
- (3) 9–10 mm red beads (optional)
- Tapestry needle
- Scissors
- (1) 8–10 mm jump ring
- Place marker

INSTEAD OF CROCHETING THE BERRIES, ATTACH 9-10 MM RED BEADS IN A CLUSTER OF THREE DIRECTLY OVER WHERE THE BOTTOM OF THE LEAVES OVERLAP.

## LEAF (MAKE 3)

With green, ch 10.

**Rnd 1:** Starting in 2nd ch from hook and working in back ridge loops, sc 8, sc 3 back ridge loop of next ch. Rotate ch so front loops are facing up. Starting in next ch and working in front loops, sc 7, sc 2 in front loop of next ch. (20 sts)

**Rnd 2:** Sl st 1, sc 1, hdc 1, (hdc 1, dc 1, ch 2, sl st in back ridge loop in 2nd ch from hook, hdc 1) in next st, sc 1, (sc 1, hdc 1, ch 2, sl st in back ridge loop in 2nd ch from hook, sc 1) in next st, sl st 1, (sl st 1, sc 1, ch 2, sl st in back ridge loop in 2nd ch from hook, sl st 1) in next st, sl st 1, (sl st 1, ch 2, sl st in back ridge loop in 2nd ch from hook, sl st 1) in next st, sl st 1, (sl st 1, sc 1, ch 2, sl st in back ridge loop in 2nd ch from hook, sl st 1) in next st, sl st 1, (sc 1, hdc 1, ch 2, sl st in back ridge loop in 2nd ch from hook, sc 1) in next st, sc 1, (hdc 1, dc 1, ch 2, sl st in back ridge loop in 2nd ch from hook, hdc 1) in next st, hdc 1, sc 1, sl st 2, ch 2, sl st in back ridge loop in 2nd ch from hook. Fasten off.

Overlap and sew the bottom tip of the leaves tog in a grouping of three.

## BERRY (MAKE 3)

With red, make a 4-st adjustable ring.

**Rnd 1:** Sc 2 in each st around. (8 sts)

**Rnd 2:** Sc 8.

**Rnd 3:** Sc2tog 4 times. (4 sts)

Fasten off.

Attach the berries in a cluster of three directly over where the bottom of the leaves overlap.

Sew on a jump ring. Add a hanger (page 18).

# MISTLETOE

······· DIFFICULTY: EASY * FINISHED SIZE: 2 1/2" (6 CM) TALL BUNDLE ·······

## ⇌ MATERIALS ⇌

- Sock weight yarn in green
- Hook size C (2.75 mm)
- Polyester fiberfill
- (17–20) 4 mm white beads
- 8" (20 cm) length of 3/8" (10 mm) red ribbon
- Tapestry needle
- Scissors
- (1) 8–10 mm jump ring
- Place marker

> You can always make the base stem for each stalk longer or shorter if you like.

### 2-LEAF STEM (MAKE 4)

Unless otherwise noted, always work in the back ridge loops of the ch. Change up the initial length of the ch (6, 7, 8, or 9 sts) for some added variation as you work.

With green, ch 6/7/8/9 for "stem" ch, ch 6, hdc 3 in 2nd ch from hook, hdc 1, sc 1, sl st 2, ch 6, hdc 3 in 2nd ch from hook, hdc 1, sc 1, sl st 2, sl st to end of stem.

Fasten off. Weave in all yarn tails.

### 4-LEAF STEM (MAKE 3)

Unless otherwise noted, always work in the back ridge loops of the ch. Change up the initial length of the ch (8, 9, or 10 sts) for some added variation as you work.

With green, ch 8/9/10 for "stem" ch, ch 6, hdc 3 in 2nd ch from hook, hdc 1, sc 1, sl st 2, ch 5 for "stem" ch, ch 6, hdc 3 in 2nd ch from hook, hdc 1, sc 1, sl st 2, ch 6, hdc 3 in 2nd ch from hook, hdc 1, sc 1, sl st 2, sl st in st at base of ch-6 leaf, sl st 5 in stem ch, ch 6, hdc 3 in 2nd ch from hook, hdc 1, sc 1, sl st 2, sl st in the stem ch at base of ch-6, sl st to end of beginning stem. Fasten off.

Weave in all yarn tails.

### BOW

Bundle the ends of the stems tog and sew tog with green yarn. Tie a red ribbon around the bundled stems and finish with a bow. To keep ribbon from fraying, dab a light coating of craft glue to the back of the ribbon ends.

### BERRIES

Sew the white beads in clusters of 2 to 3 to the stems at the points where the pairs of leaves meet.

Sew on a jump ring. Add a hanger (page 18).

# POINSETTIA

······ DIFFICULTY: EASY * FINISHED SIZE: 2 1/2" TALL, 2 1/2" WIDE (6 X 6 CM) ·······

## ⋡ MATERIALS ⋡

- Sock weight yarn in green and red
- Hook size C (2.75 mm)
- Polyester fiberfill
- (9) 6/0 "E" yellow seed beads
- Tapestry needle
- Invisible thread
- Scissors
- (1) 8–10 mm jump ring
- Place marker

## RED PETALS (MAKE 2)

With red, make a 6-st adjustable ring.

**Rnd 1:** *Sl st 1, ch 7, starting in 2nd ch from hook and working in back ridge loops, sl st 6; rep from * 5 more times.

**Rnd 2:** *Sl st 2, ch 2, hdc 2, sc 1, sl st 1, (sl st 1, ch 2, sl st 1) at the top of the ch. Working down other side of ch, sl st 1, sc 1, hdc 2, ch 2, sl st; rep from * 5 more times. (6 petals)

Fasten off, leaving a long tail for sewing.

## GREEN CENTER

With green, make a 6-st adjustable ring.

**Rnd 1:** *Sc 1, sc2tog; rep from * 1 more time. (4 sts)

Fasten off, leaving a long tail for sewing.

## GREEN LEAVES

With green, make a 12-st adjustable ring.

**Rnd 1:** *Sl st 2, ch 9, starting in 2nd ch from hook and working in back ridge loops, sl st 8; rep from * 5 more times.

**Rnd 2:** *Sl st 3, ch 2, hdc 3, sc 2, sl st 1, (sl st 1, ch 2, sl st 1) at the top of the ch. Starting in next st and working down opposite side of ch, sl st 1, sc 2, hdc 3, ch 2, sl st 1; rep from * 5 more times. (6 petals)

Fasten off, leaving a long tail for sewing.

Layer, offset, and sew the middle of the red petals tog. Sew the green leaves to the bottom of the red petals. Sew the open edge of the green center to middle of flower (sewing through all 3 layers to secure). Sew yellow beads to the green center of the flower.

Sew on a jump ring. Add a hanger (page 18).

# CHRISTMAS PICKLE

······ DIFFICULTY: EASY * FINISHED SIZE: 2 3/4" TALL, 1 1/2" WIDE (7 X 4 CM) ······

## ⇌ MATERIALS ⇌

- Sock weight yarn in green
- Hook size C (2.75 mm)
- Polyester fiberfill
- Tapestry needle
- Scissors
- (1) 8–10 mm jump ring
- Place marker

HOW TO MAKE PICKLE BOBBLES:

YO, INSERT HOOK INTO NEXT ST, AND DRAW UP A LOOSE LOOP. YO AND DRAW YARN THROUGH FIRST 2 LOOPS ON HOOK. YOU WILL HAVE 2 LOOPS REMAINING ON YOUR HOOK.

*YO, INSERT HOOK INTO CURRENT ST, AND DRAW UP A LOOSE LOOP. YO AND DRAW YARN THROUGH FIRST 2 LOOPS ON HOOK; REP FROM * 1 MORE TIME. YOU WILL HAVE 4 LOOPS REMAINING ON YOUR HOOK.

YO AND DRAW YARN THROUGH THE 4 LOOPS ON THE HOOK TO COMPLETE THE BOBBLE.

## PICKLE

With green, make a 6-st adjustable ring.

**Rnd 1:** Sc 2 in each st around. (12 sts)

**Rnd 2:** *Sc 1, sc 2 in next st; rep from * 5 more times. (18 sts)

For rnds 3–19, intermittently replace some sc sts for bobbles (see tip below), randomly applying 0,1, or 2 bobbles per rnd. By rnd 19, you will have 15 to 20 bobbles in total on the surface of the pickle.

**Rnds 3–14:** Sc 18.

**Rnd 15:** *Sc 4, sc2tog; rep from * 2 more times. (15 sts)

**Rnds 16–19:** Sc 15.

**Rnd 20:** *Sc 3, sc2tog; rep from * 2 more times. (12 sts)

Stuff pickle.

**Rnd 21:** Sc2tog 6 times. (6 sts)

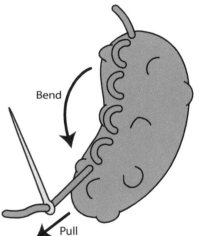

Bend

Pull

Fasten off, leaving a long yarn tail for sewing.

Close hole in smaller end of pickle. Apply a line of running stitches along one side of the pickle from the small end to the larger end. Pull the yarn gently to curve the pickle. Fasten off tail at the larger end.

Sew on a jump ring to the larger end of the pickle. Add a hanger (page 18).

# THE NUTCRACKER

*G*ot a little sugarplum fairy in your life? Been to *Nutcracker* recitals so many times you know all the steps by heart? Does the "Waltz of the Flowers" get stuck in your head every December? Then this set is for you! Now Clara, the Nutcracker, the Sugar Plum Fairy, and even the Mouse King can dance around your tree just in time for the holidays.

# SUGARPLUM FAIRY

······· DIFFICULTY: INTERMEDIATE • FINISHED SIZE: 3" TALL, 1 1/2" WIDE (8 X 4 CM) ·······

## ⇌ MATERIALS ⇌

- Sock weight yarn in blue violet, dark purple, green, light purple, tan, and white
- Hook size C (2.75 mm)
- Tapestry needle
- Scissors
- Polyester fiberfill
- Craft glue or needle and thread
- (1) 8–10 mm jump ring
- Place marker

## HEAD AND BODY

With tan yarn, make a 6-st adjustable ring.

**Rnd 1:** Sc 2 in each st around. (12 sts)

**Rnd 2:** *Sc 2, sc 2 in next st; rep from * 3 more times. (16 sts)

**Rnds 3–5:** Sc 16.

**Rnd 6:** *Sc 2, sc2tog; rep from * 3 more times. (12 sts)

Stuff head.

**Rnd 7:** Sc2tog 6 times. (6 sts)

Cut tan. Change to dark purple.

**Rnd 8:** In bl, *sc 2, sc 2 in next st; rep from * 1 more time. (8 sts)

**Rnd 9:** *Sc 3, sc 2 in next st; rep from * 1 more time. (10 sts)

**Rnd 10:** *Sc 4, sc 2 in next st; rep from * 1 more time. (12 sts)

**Rnd 11:** *Sc 5, sc 2 in next st; rep from * 1 more time. (14 sts)

**Rnd 12:** *Sc 6, sc 2 in next st; rep from * 1 more time. (16 sts)

**Rnd 13:** BPsc 16.

**Rnd 14:** *Sc 2, sc2tog; rep from * 3 more times. (12 sts)

Stuff body.

**Rnd 15:** Sc2tog 6 times. (6 sts)

Fasten off, close hole, and weave in end.

## COLLAR DETAIL

**Rnd 1:** With head pointed up and using dark purple yarn, (sl st 1, ch 1, sc 1) in one of the exposed fls above rnd 8. Cont to work 5 more sc sts into the exposed fls. (6 sts)

Fasten off and weave in end.

## TUTU DETAIL

**Rnd 1:** With head pointing down and using light purple yarn, (sl st 1, ch 3, sl st 1) in the fl of one exposed BP sts from rnd 13. Cont to work in just the fl (sl st 1, ch 3, sl st 1) in each of the next 15 exposed stitches of rnd 13. (Results in 16 ch-3 loops.)

**Rnd 2:** Working in just the bl of the exposed BP sts from rnd

# SUGARPLUM FAIRY (continued)

13, (sl st 1, ch 3, sl st 1) in each st around. (Results in 16 ch-3 loops.)

Fasten off and weave in end.

## ARM (MAKE 2)

With tan, make a 3-st adjustable ring.

**Rnd 1:** Sc 2 in each st around. (6 sts)

**Rnds 2–5:** Sc 6.

Fasten off.

Close hole at the top of the arm and sew to the shoulders of the body.

## LEG (MAKE 2)

With blue violet yarn, make a 3-st adjustable ring.

**Rnd 1:** Sc 2 in each st around. (6 sts)

**Rnd 2:** Sc 6.

Cut blue violet. Change to white.

**Rnds 3–5:** Sc 6.

Fasten off. Stuff leg lightly. Attach open edges of legs to the hips of the body under the tutu. Sew the sides of the feet tog.

## PLUM BLOSSOM HAT

With green, make a 5-st adjustable ring.

**Rnd 1:** BPsc 5.

Cut green. Change to light purple.

**Rnd 2:** Sc 2 in each st around. (10 sts)

**Rnd 3:** *Sl st 1, (sl st 1, ch 2, hdc 1, dc 1, hdc 1, ch 2, sl st 1) in next st; rep from * 4 more times. (5 petals)

**Rnd 4:** *Sl st 1, sl st 2 in ch-2 sp, sc 1, (hdc 1, ch 2, sl st in back ridge loop of 2nd ch from hook, hdc 1) in next st, sc 1, sl st 2 in ch-2 sp; rep from * 4 more times. (5 petals)

Fasten off, leaving a long tail for sewing.

## STEM DETAIL

With green, ch 4.

Fasten off and weave yarn tail down through the ch-4 to the base. Attach stem to green part of blossom.

Place blossom stem side up on top of head and sew in place.

## WINGS

**Rnd 1:** With white, ch 6 and sl st in back ridge loop of 6th ch from hook, *ch 4, sl st in back ridge loop of st at the base of ch 4; rep from * 1 more time, ch 6, sl st in back ridge loop of st at the base of ch 6. (Results in 2 ch-6 sps, 2 ch-4 sps.)

**Rnd 2:** (Sl st 1, sc 2, hdc 2, ch 2, hdc 2, sc 2, sl st 1) in ch-6 sp, (sl st 1, sc 4, sl st 1) in next 2 ch-4 sps, (sl st 1, sc 2, hdc 2, ch 2, hdc 2, sc 2, sl st 1) in ch-6 sp.

Fasten off, leaving a long tail for sewing.

Sew middle of wings to back of fairy body.

Sew on a jump ring behind the blossom hat stem. Add a hanger (page 18).

# NUTCRACKER

······ DIFFICULTY: INTERMEDIATE * FINISHED SIZE: 3 1/2" TALL, 2" WIDE (9 X 5 CM) ······

## ⨝ MATERIALS ⨝

- Sock weight yarn in black, gold, ivory, red, tan, and white
- Hook size C (2.75 mm)
- Tapestry needle
- Scissors
- Felt in black, gold/yellow, and white
- (1) 6 mm gold metallic bead
- Polyester fiberfill
- (6) 6/0 "E" silver seed beads
- Beading needle
- Invisible thread
- Black thread
- Craft glue or needle and thread
- (1) 8–10 mm jump ring
- Place marker

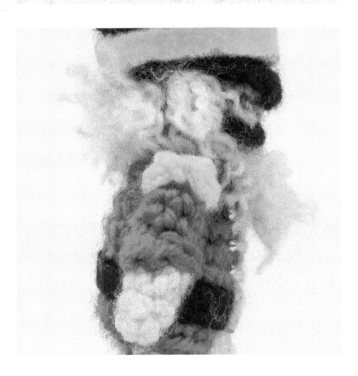

## HEAD AND BODY

With tan yarn, make a 6-st adjustable ring.

**Rnd 1:** Sc 2 in each st around. (12 sts)

**Rnd 2:** *Sc 2, sc 2 in next st; rep from * 3 more times. (16 sts)

**Rnds 3–5:** Sc 16.

**Rnd 6:** *Sc 2, sc2tog; rep from * 3 more times. (12 sts)

Stuff head.

Cut tan. Change to red.

**Rnd 7:** FPsc 12.

**Rnd 8:** *Sl st 2, hdc 2 in next st, hdc 1, hdc 2 in next st, sl st 1; rep from * 1 more time. (16 sts)

**Rnd 9:** BPsc 16.

**Rnds 10–12:** Sc 16.

**Rnd 13:** BPsc 16.

Stuff body.

**Rnd 14:** Sc2tog 8 times. (8 sts)

Fasten off, close hole, and weave in end.

## JACKET DETAIL

**Rnd 1:** With head pointed up and using red yarn, (sl st 1, ch 1, sc 1) at the back of the body in one of the rnd 13 exposed loops. Cont to work 15 more sc sts into the exposed loops of rnd 13. (16 sts)

Fasten off and weave in end.

## HAND AND ARM (MAKE 2)

With white yarn, make a 3-st adjustable ring.

**Rnd 1:** Sc 2 in each st around. (6 sts)

**Rnds 2–3:** Sc 6.

Stuff hand.

Cut white. Change to red.

**Rnd 4:** FPsc 6.

# NUTCRACKER *(continued)*

**Rnd 5:** In bl, sc 6.

**Rnds 6–7:** Sc 6.

Cut red. Change to gold.

**Rnd 8:** FPsc 6.

Fasten off. Weave yarn tail through bl of rnd 8 and pull to close.

## SLEEVE DETAIL

**Rnd 1:** With hand pointed up and using red yarn, (sl st 1, ch 1, sc 1) in one of the exposed fl above rnd 4. Cont to work 5 more sc sts into the exposed fl. (6 sts)

Fasten off and weave in end.

## SHOULDER CAP DETAIL

**Rnd 1:** With hand pointed up and using gold yarn, (sl st 1, ch 1, sc 1) in one of the rnd 8 exposed fls. Cont to work 5 more sc sts into the exposed fls of rnd 3. (6 sts)

Fasten off and weave in end. Push shoulder cap down to cover upper arm.

Sew side of shoulder caps to the shoulders of the body (the shoulders are indicated by the hdc stitches on rnd 8 on the body). With red yarn, tack the inside surfaces of the arms to the body to keep them from splaying out.

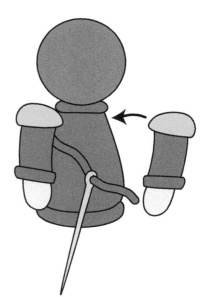

## LEG (MAKE 2)

With black yarn, make a 6-st adjustable ring.

**Rnd 1:** In bl, sc 2, ch 3, sk ch-3, sk 3, sc 1. (6 sts)

**Rnd 2:** Sc 2, sc in each ch of ch-3, sc 1. (6 sts)

**Rnd 3:** Sc 6.

Cut black. Change to white.

**Rnd 4:** In bl, sc 6.

**Rnd 5:** Sc 6.

Fasten off, leaving a long tail for sewing.

## BOOT TOE DETAIL

**Rnd 1:** With black and starting in lower right corner of boot opening, reattach black yarn (sl st, ch 1, sc 1) to rejoin yarn (counts as first sc). Cont to sc in the remaining 5 sts around the inside of the boot opening. (6 sts)

**Rnd 2:** Sc 6.

# NUTCRACKER *(continued)*

Fasten off, leaving a long tail. Lightly stuff boot and leg and close hole. Use leftover yarn tail to patch any holes in the sides of the boot.

## BOOT CUFF DETAIL

**Rnd 1:** With boot pointed down and using black, (sl st 1, ch 1, sc 1) in one of the rnd 4 exposed fls. Cont to work 5 more sc sts into the exposed fls of rnd 4. (6 sts)

Fasten off and weave in end. Fold boot cuff down.

Sew open edges of legs to the bottom of the body.

## HAT

With black, make a 6-st adjustable ring.

**Rnd 1:** Sc 2 in each st around. (12 sts)

**Rnd 2:** *Sc 1, sc 2 in next st; rep from * 5 more times. (18 sts)

**Rnd 3:** *Sc 2, sc 2 in next st; rep from * 5 more times. (24 sts)

**Rnd 4:** BPsc 24.

**Rnd 5:** *Sc 10, sc2tog; rep from * 1 more time. (22 sts)

**Rnd 6:** *Sc 9, sc2tog; rep from * 1 more time. (20 sts)

**Rnd 7:** *Sc 8, sc2tog; rep from * 1 more time. (18 sts)

**Rnd 8:** Sc 18.

**Rnd 9:** Sl st 6, in fl, sl st 1, sc 1, hdc 2 in next 2 sts, sc 1, sl st 1, in tbl, sl st 6.

Fasten off.

Place a small amount of stuffing into the hat and pull the hat halfway down onto the head with the brim detail from rnd 9 at the front. Sew the edge of the hat to the head. Thread the leftover yarn tail up through the top of the hat and back down, exiting at the base of the hat in the back, pulling gently to flatten the top of the hat. Fasten off.

With beading needle and invisible thread, sew a 6 mm gold metallic bead to the top of the hat.

## FELT PARTS

Cut out one jacket panel from white felt. It should be 1" (3 cm) tall, 1/4" (6 mm) wide in the middle, and curve out to 1/2" (13 mm) wide at the top and bottom. Glue or sew to front of jacket.

From black felt, cut out (1) 1/4" x 3 1/4" (6 mm x 8 cm) strip. Wrap around jacket for a belt, trim to fit, and secure the ends in the back.

With gold yarn, apply 3 long parallel stitches across the jacket panel above the belt. With invisible thread and beading thread, apply 1 silver seed bead to each end of the gold long stitches across the chest.

From gold/yellow felt, cut out (1) 1/4" x 3 1/4" (6 mm x 8 cm) strip and (1) 1/4" x 3/8" (6 x 10 mm) rectangle. Attach the rectangle to the front of the belt as a buckle. Wrap the strip around the hat above the brim, trim to fit, and secure the ends in the back.

From white felt, cut out (1) 1/2" x 1/4" (13 x 6 mm) rectangle. Put aside for teeth.

## BEARD AND TEETH

Cut (6) 4" (10 cm) pieces of ivory yarn and attach them using fringe knots in a cluster at the bottom of the chin with the red rnd directly below the chin. Separate yarn plies with the tapestry needle, fluff with

your fingers, and trim to desired length. Flatten/smooth down beard. Attach the felt for the teeth over the knots at the base of the fringe with a bit of glue. Double up a piece of black thread on a sewing needle and apply 3 vertical and 1 horizontal long stitch over the felt to define separate teeth.

## HAIR AND MUSTACHE

Cut (8) 5" (13 cm) pieces of ivory yarn and attach them using fringe knots just under the bottom of the hat around the back of the head. Separate yarn plies with the tapestry needle, fluff with your fingers, and trim to desired length.

With black yarn, apply 3 droopy long stitches from the middle of the head above the teeth to the side of the cheek for half a mustache. Repeat on other cheek for 2nd half of mustache.

Sew on a jump ring. Add a hanger (page 18).

# CLARA

## ⇌ MATERIALS ⇌

- Sock weight yarn in brown, light yellow, magenta, tan, and white
- Hook size C (2.75 mm)
- Tapestry needle
- Scissors
- Polyester fiberfill
- (1) 8–10 mm jump ring
- Place marker

## HEAD AND BODY

With tan yarn, make a 6-st adjustable ring.

**Rnd 1:** Sc 2 in each st around. (12 sts)

**Rnd 2:** *Sc 2, sc 2 in next st; rep from * 3 more times. (16 sts)

**Rnds 3–5:** Sc 16.

**Rnd 6:** *Sc 2, sc2tog; rep from * 3 more times. (12 sts)

Stuff head.

**Rnd 7:** Sc2tog 6 times. (6 sts)

Cut tan. Change to light yellow.

**Rnd 8:** In bl, *sc 2, sc 2 in next st; rep from * 1 more time. (8 sts)

**Rnd 9:** *Sc 3, sc 2 in next st; rep from * 1 more time. (10 sts)

**Rnd 10:** *Sc 4, sc 2 in next st; rep from * 1 more time. (12 sts)

**Rnds 11–12:** Sc 12.

**Rnd 13:** *Sc 5, sc 2 in next st; rep from * 1 more time. (14 sts)

**Rnd 14:** Sc 14.

**Rnd 15:** *Sc 6, sc 2 in next st; rep from * 1 more time. (16 sts)

**Rnd 16:** *Sc 7, sc 2 in next st; rep from * 1 more time. (18 sts)

**Rnd 17:** BPsc 18.

Stuff body.

**Rnd 18:** Sc2tog 9 times. (9 sts)

Fasten off, stuff body, close hole, and weave in end.

## COLLAR DETAIL

**Rnd 1:** With head pointed up and using light yellow yarn, (sl st 1, ch 1, sc 1) in one of the exposed fls above rnd 8. Cont to work 5 more sc sts into the exposed fls. (6 sts)

Fasten off and weave in end.

# CLARA *(continued)*

## SKIRT DETAIL

**Rnd 1:** With head pointing down and using light yellow yarn, (sl st 1, ch 1, sc 1) in one exposed st from rnd 17, *sc 2 in next exposed st, sc 1; rep from * 7 more times, sc 2 in rem exposed sts from rnd 17. (27 sts)

**Rnd 2:** Sc 27.

Fasten off and weave in end.

## LEGS (MAKE 2)

With magenta yarn, make a 3-st adjustable ring.

**Rnd 1:** Sc 2 in each st around. (6 sts)

**Rnd 2:** Sc 6.

Cut magenta. Change to white.

**Rnds 3–4:** Sc 6.

Fasten off. Stuff leg lightly.

Attach open edges of legs to bottom of body.

## HAND AND ARM (MAKE 2)

With tan yarn, make a 3-st adjustable ring.

**Rnd 1:** Sc 2 in each st around. (6 sts)

**Rnd 2:** *Sc 1, sc2tog; rep from * 1 more time. (4 sts)

Cut tan. Change to light yellow.

**Rnd 3:** FPsc 4.

**Rnd 4:** Sc 2 in each st around. (8 sts)

**Rnd 5:** In bl, sc 8.

**Rnd 6:** Sc 8.

**Rnd 7:** *Sc 2, sc2tog; rep from * 1 more time. (6 sts)

Fasten off and stuff arm lightly. Close hole at top of shoulder.

## SLEEVE DETAIL

**Rnd 1:** With hand pointed up and using light yellow yarn, (sl st 1, ch 1, sc 1) in one of the rnd 5 exposed fl. Cont to work 7 more sc sts into the exposed fls. (8 sts)

**Rnd 2:** Sc 8.

Fasten off and weave in end.

Sew the shoulders to the sides of the body on either side of the neck.

## HAIR

With brown, make an 8-st adjustable ring.

**Rnd 1:** Sc 2 in each st around. (16 sts)

**Rnd 2:** *Sc 3, sc 2 in next st; rep from * 3 more times. (20 sts)

**Rnd 3:** (Sl st 1, hdc 2) in next st, (hdc 1, sc 1) in next st, sl st 1, (sc 1, hdc 1) in next st, (hdc 2, sl st 1) in next st, sk 1, sl st 1, sk 1, sl st 1, hdc 2 in next 7 sts, sl st 1, sk 1, sl st 1, sk 1. (29 sts)

**Rnd 4:** Sl st 1, sc 4, sl st 1, sc 4, sl st 1, sk 2, sl st 1, hdc 2 in next st, hdc 10, hdc 2 in next st, sl st 1, sk 2 and fasten off in next st. (27 sts)

Fasten off, leaving a long tail for sewing.

Place hair on head and sew edge of hair to the temples and front of the forehead. Leave the back of the hair loose.

## HAIR BAND

With magenta, ch 10 and fasten off. Stretch the hair band over the top of the hair and sew the ends of the hair band to the temples of the head, under the hairline.

## SASH

With magenta yarn, ch 26 and fasten off. Wrap ch around the chest of the body and tie in a square knot in back. Trim yarn tails fairly short and separate yarn plies with tapestry needle or your fingers.

Sew on a jump ring. Add a hanger (page 18).

# MOUSE KING

······ DIFFICULTY: INTERMEDIATE * FINISHED SIZE: 3 1/4" TALL, 1 1/2" WIDE (8 X 4 CM) ······

## ⇌ MATERIALS ⇌

- Sock weight yarn in black, gold, ivory, light gray, pink, and white
- Hook size C (2.75 mm)
- Tapestry needle
- Scissors
- (1) 6 mm plastic safety eye
- Dark blue felt
- Polyester fiberfill
- (6) 6/0 "E" gold seed beads
- Craft glue or needle and thread
- (1) 8–10 mm jump ring
- Place marker

## HEAD

With light gray, make a 6-st adjustable ring.

Rnd 1: Sc 2 in each st around. (12 sts)

Rnd 2: *Sc 2, sc 2 in next st; rep from * 3 more times. (16 sts)

Rnds 3–5: Sc 16.

Rnd 6: *Sc 2, sc2tog; rep from * 3 more times. (12 sts)

Rnd 7: Sc 12.

Rnd 8: *Sc 1, sc2tog; rep from * 3 more times. (8 sts)

Stuff head.

Rnd 9: *Sc 2, sc2tog; rep from * 1 more time. (6 sts)

Fasten off and close hole.

Glue or sew a 6 mm plastic safety eye to the front of the head for a nose.

## EAR (MAKE 2)

With light gray, make a 6-st adjustable ring.

Rnd 1: Sc 2 in each st around. (12 sts)

Fasten off.

Sew ears to top corners of the head.

## CROWN

With gold, make a 6-st adjustable ring.

Rnd 1: In bl, loosely sl st 6.

Rnd 2: *(Sl st 1, ch 3, sl st 1) in next st; rep from * 5 more times.

Fasten off and sew base of crown to head between the ears.

With invisible thread and beading needle, sew gold seed beads to outside of crown, using photos for reference.

## BODY

With light gray, make a 6-st adjustable ring.

Rnd 1: Sc 2 in each st around. (12 sts)

Rnd 2: Sc 4, change to ivory, sc 4, change to light gray, sc 4, ch 1, turn. (12 sts)

Row 3: Sk ch 1, sc 3, change to ivory, sc 6, change to light gray, sc 3, ch 1, turn. (12 sts)

Row 4: Sk ch 1, sc 3, change to ivory, sc2tog, sc 2, sc2tog, change to light gray, sc 3, ch 1, turn. (10 sts)

Row 5: Sk ch 1, sc 3, change to ivory, sc 4, change to light gray, sc 3, ch 1, turn. (10 sts)

Row 6: Sk ch 1, sc 3, change to ivory, sc2tog 2 times, change to light gray, sc 3. Do not turn. (8 sts)

Hold seam edges tog and work across the gap and work in the round.

Rnd 7: Sc 8.

Rnd 8: *Sc 2, sc2tog; rep from * 1 more time. (6 sts)

Fasten off.

Stuff body and close seam in the back of the body with a whip stitch.

With light gray, apply a ch st around the edge of the ivory belly to clean up the edge.

Sew the bottom of the head to the open edge of the neck.

# MOUSE KING (continued)

## HAND AND ARM (MAKE 2)

With white yarn, make a 3-st adjustable ring.

**Rnd 1:** Sc 2 in each st around. (6 sts)

**Rnd 2:** *Sc 1, sc2tog; rep from * 1 more time. (4 sts)

Stuff hand.

Cut white. Change to light gray.

**Rnd 3:** FPsc 4.

**Rnd 4:** *Sc 1, sc 2 in next st; rep from * 1 more time. (6 sts)

**Rnds 5–6:** Sc 6.

**Rnd 7:** *Sc 1, sc2tog; rep from * 1 more time. (4 sts)

Fasten off and stuff arm lightly. Close hole at top of arm.

Sew the arms to the shoulders of the body. With white yarn, tack the hands to the sides of the hips.

## LEG (MAKE 2)

With black yarn, make a 6-st adjustable ring.

**Rnd 1:** In bl, sc 2, ch 3, sk ch-3, sk 3, sc 1. (6 sts)

**Rnd 2:** Sc 2, sc in each ch of ch-3, sc 1. (6 sts)

**Rnd 3:** Sc 6.

Cut black. Change to light gray.

**Rnd 4:** In bl, sc 6.

**Rnd 5:** Sc 6.

Fasten off, leaving a long tail for sewing.

## BOOT TOE DETAIL

**Rnd 1:** With black and starting in lower right corner of boot opening, reattach black yarn (sl st, ch 1, sc 1) to rejoin yarn (counts as first sc). Cont to sc in the remaining 5 sts around the inside of the boot opening. (6 sts)

**Rnd 2:** Sc 6.

Fasten off, leaving a long tail. Lightly stuff boot and leg and close hole. Use leftover yarn tail to patch any holes in the sides of the boot.

## BOOT CUFF DETAIL

**Rnd 1:** With boot pointed down and using black yarn, (sl st 1, ch 1, sc 1) in one of the rnd 4 exposed fl. Cont to work 5 more sc sts into the exposed fl. (6 sts)

Fasten off and weave in end. Fold boot cuff down.

Sew open edges of legs to the bottom of the body.

## TAIL

With pink, make a 4-st adjustable ring.

**Rnd 1:** In bl, sc 4.

**Rnd 2:** In bl, sc 1, sk 1, sc 2. (3 sts)

Cont to sc around in the bl until tail measures 1 1/2" (4 cm) long.

Attach tail to back of body.

## SASH

Cut (1) 5" x 3/8" (13 cm x 10 mm) strip of dark blue felt. Drape the felt over one shoulder and overlap the ends of the strip at the hip on the opposite side of the body. Glue or sew the felt in place at the overlap point. Trim the ends short.

Sew on a jump ring. Add a hanger (page 18).

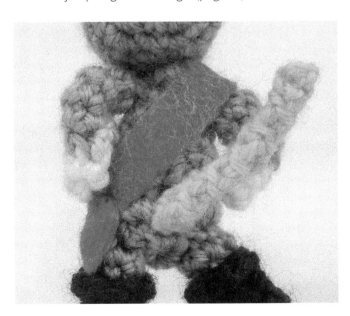

# GIFTS FROM SANTA

*A*round the Christmas tree and nestled in the stockings on the mantle, Santa leaves special treats for all the good little children sleeping soundly in their beds: puffing train engines, wooden rocking horses, smiling rag dolls, toasty socks, and furry friends in festive gift boxes tied with silvery bows eagerly anticipating the excitement of Christmas morning. Just watch out for that occasional lump of coal!

GIFTS FROM SANTA

# TRAIN ENGINE

DIFFICULTY: INTERMEDIATE * FINISHED SIZE: 2 1/2" TALL, 3" LONG (6 X 8 CM)

## MATERIALS

- Sock weight yarn in black, gold, gray, green, red, and white
- Hook size C (2.75 mm)
- Tapestry needle
- Scissors
- (1) 1/4" (6 mm) gold bead
- (6) 6/0 "E" silver seed beads
- Invisible thread
- White thread
- Beading needle
- Stabilizer foam (optional)
- Polyester fiberfill
- (1) 8–10 mm jump ring
- Place marker

## CAB

### Base

With green, make an 8-st adjustable ring.

**Rnd 1:** *Sc 1, (sc 1, hdc 1, sc 1) in next st; rep from * 3 more times. (16 sts)

**Rnd 2:** *Sc 2, (sc 1, hdc 1, pm, sc 1) in next st, sc 1; rep from * 3 more times. (24 sts)

**Fasten off.**

Keep marker in place as you work side walls.

### Side wall

**Row 1:** With RS of work facing up and starting with green yarn, (sl st 1, ch 1, sc 1) in bl in any marked st. Cont working in bl and sc 6 to next marker, turn, ch 1. Leave all markers in place. (7 sts)

**Rows 2–4:** Sk ch, sc 7, turn, ch 1. (7 sts)

**Row 5:** Sk ch, sc 1, cut green yarn, leaving a 24" (61 cm) tail at the back of your work, change to white yarn, sc 5, reattach green yarn from skein, sc 1, turn, ch 1. (7 sts)

Take care to keep all yarn tails on the same side of your work as you work the next rows.

**Rows 6–8:** Sk ch, sc 1, change to white, sc 5, change to green, sc 1, turn, ch 1. (7 sts)

Cut white yarn.

**Row 9:** Sk ch, sc 7, turn, ch 1. (7 sts)

**Row 10:** Sk ch, sc 7. (7 sts)

Fasten off.

Hold the cab with RS facing up. All the yarn tails will be at the back of your work.

### Back wall

**Row 1:** With green yarn, insert hook into the bl of marked st at the lower left corner of the side wall, (sl st 1, ch 1, sc 1) in

# TRAIN ENGINE *(continued)*

bl of marked st. Cont working in bl and sc 6 to next marker, turn. Leave all markers in place. (7 sts)

Repeat side wall steps from row 2 to end.

**Rows 2–9:** Sk ch, sc 7, turn, ch 1. (7 sts)

**Row 10:** Sk ch, sc 7. (7 sts)

Fasten off.

## 2nd side wall

**Row 1:** With green yarn, insert hook into the bl of marked st at the lower left corner of your back wall, (sl st 1, ch 1, sc 1) in bl of marked st. Cont working in bl and sc 6 to next marker, turn. Leave all markers in place. (7 sts)

Repeat side wall steps from row 2 to end.

Hold the cab with RS facing up. All the yarn tails will be at the back of your work.

## Front wall

**Row 1:** With green yarn, insert hook into the bl of marked st at the lower left corner of your side wall, (sl st 1, ch 1, sc 1) in

bl of marked st. Cont working in bl and sc 6 to next marker, turn. Leave all markers in place. (7 sts)

Repeat back wall steps from row 2 to end.

## Top

Make a 2nd base without the markers and put aside for a cab top.

## Assembly

With WS facing out, hold each pair of wall edges tog. Starting at the top corner and working through the side edge of both walls, (sl st, ch 1, sc 1) to reattach yarn and sc the matching side edges tog from top to bottom. Rep on the other 3 matching edges.

Turn cab RS out.

Stuff with squares of foam or fiberfill stuffing. Line up corners and sew cab top to open edge of cab to make a cube shape.

With red yarn and embroidery needle, embroider a line of chain stitches around the border of the white rectangles on the wide walls of the cab.

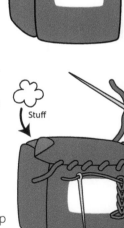

## ROOF

With black, make an 8-st adjustable ring.

**Rnd 1:** *Sc 1, (sc 1, hdc 1, sc 1) in next st; rep from * 3 more times. (16 sts)

**Rnd 2:** *Sc 2, (sc 1, hdc 1, pm, sc 1) in next st, sc 1; rep from * 3 more times. (24 sts)

**Rnd 3:** *Sc 3, (sc 1, hdc 1, pm, sc 1) in next st, sc 2; rep from * 3 more times. (32 sts)

**Rnd 4:** *Sc 4, (sc 1, hdc 1, pm, sc 1) in next st, sc 3; rep from * 3 more times. (40 sts)

**Rnd 5:** BPsc 40.

Fasten off.

Place roof on top of cab with the rnd 5 edge overhanging the top edge of the cab. With black yarn, sew rnd 4 of roof around the top edge of cab. Add a bit of stuffing to puff up the roof before closing the seam. To give the roof a domed look, run black yarn back and forth through rnd 4 from one side edge of the roof to the other, pulling gently to shape the center of the roof into a slight dome.

## BOILER

With gray yarn, make a 10-st adjustable ring.

**Rnd 1:** Sc 2 in each st around. (20 sts)

**Rnd 2:** BPsc 20.

Cut gray yarn. Change to green.

**Rnds 3–9:** Sc 20.

**Rnd 10:** In bl, sc 20.

**Rnd 11:** Sc2tog 10 times. (10 sts)

Stuff boiler and close hole.

Line up bottom edges of the boiler and cab. With green, sew back end of boiler to front of cab wall.

## CHIMNEY

With black, make an 8-st adjustable ring.

**Rnd 1:** In bl, sc 8.

**Rnd 2:** *Sc 1, sc 2 in next st; rep from * 3 more times. (12 sts)

**Rnd 3:** Sc 12.

**Rnd 4:** *Sc 1, sc 2 in next st, sc 1; rep from * 3 more times. (16 sts)

**Rnd 5:** Sc 16.

**Rnd 6:** BPsc 16.

**Rnd 7:** *Sc 1, sc2tog, sc 1; rep from * 3 more times. (12 sts)

Stuff chimney.

**Rnd 8:** In bl, sc2tog 6 times. (6 sts)

Fasten off.

Close hole at top of chimney and draw yarn tail down through the chimney to help flatten down the top of the shape.

## BOILER RIM DETAIL (MAKE 4)

With gold yarn, ch 16 (or adjust to boiler size as necessary).

Wrap 3 of the ch-16 around rnds 3, 7, and 10 of the boiler (i.e., the front edge, middle, and where the boiler meets the cab). Tie ch ends tog and secure where the ends meet underneath the boiler. It should be snug and cause the boiler to bulge a bit.

Wrap 4th ch around rnd 5 of chimney (directly below the ridge on rnd 6). Secure and sew in yarn tails.

With black, sew the base of the chimney to the top front half of the boiler between first and 2nd rim detail ch.

With invisible thread and a beading needle, sew (1) 1/4" (6 mm) gold metal bead to the front of the boiler.

# TRAIN ENGINE *(continued)*

## LARGE WHEEL (MAKE 4)

With gray, make an 8-st adjustable ring.

**Rnd 1:** Sc 2 in each st around. (16 sts)

**Rnd 2:** BPsc 16.

Sl st in next st to fasten off.

With ridge detail facing out, sew a pair of large wheels to each side of train cab. With invisible thread and a beading needle, sew a small silver 6/0 "E" bead to the middle of each wheel.

## SMALL WHEEL (MAKE 2)

With gray, make a 10-st adjustable ring.

**Rnd 1:** (Sl st 1, BPsc 1) in next st, BPsc 9.

Sl st in next st to fasten off.

With ridge detail facing out, sew one small wheel to the sides of the front half of the boiler. With invisible thread and a beading needle, sew a small silver 6/0 "E" bead to the middle of each wheel.

## COW CATCHER

With red, make a 6-st adjustable ring, ch 1, turn. Do not join ring. Work rows in a semi-circle shape.

**Row 1:** Sk ch, hdc 2 in next st, sc 4, hdc 2 in next st, ch 1, turn. (8 sts)

**Row 2:** Sk ch, FPsc 8. (8 sts)

Sl st to fasten off.

Attach flat edge of cow catcher to bottom front edge of boiler.

## SMOKE

Take a small wisp of fiberfill (about 2" [5 cm] long) and lay over the top of the chimney. With white thread, attach the center of wisp to the top of chimney by looping the thread over the middle of the fiberfill 4 to 5 times before fastening off the thread. Tease the ends of the wisp up.

Sew on a jump ring. Add a hanger (page 18).

# PUPPY IN SQUARE GIFT BOX

····· DIFFICULTY: INTERMEDIATE * FINISHED SIZE: 3" TALL, 3" LONG (8 X 8 CM) ·······

## ⥻ MATERIALS ⥻

- Sock weight yarn in black, blue, gray, tan, and white
- Hook size C (2.75 mm)
- Tapestry needle
- Black embroidery thread/floss
- Scissors
- 1/4" (6 mm) ribbon
- (2) 4 mm plastic eyes
- Polyester fiberfill
- 8" (20 cm) square of blue felt
- Craft glue or needle and thread
- (1) 8–10 mm jump ring
- Place marker

## BOX BASE

With blue yarn, make a 4-st adjustable ring.

**Rnd 1:** Sc 3 in each st around. (12 sts)

**Rnd 2:** *Sc 1, sc 3 in next st, sc 1; rep from * 3 more times. (20 sts)

**Rnd 3:** *Sc 2, sc 3 in next st, sc 2; rep from * 3 more times. (28 sts)

**Rnd 4:** BPsc 28.

**Rnds 5–11:** Sc 28.

Fasten off.

## BOX LID

With blue yarn, make a 4-st adjustable ring.

**Rnd 1:** Sc 3 in each st around. (12 sts)

**Rnd 2:** *Sc 1, sc 3 in next st, sc 1; rep from * 3 more times. (20 sts)

**Rnd 3:** *Sc 2, sc 3 in next st, sc 2; rep from * 3 more times. (28 sts)

**Rnd 4:** *Sc 3, sc 3 in next st, sc 3; rep from * 3 more times. (36 sts)

**Rnd 5:** BPsc 36.

**Rnds 6–7:** Sc 36.

Fasten off.

## FELT

From blue felt, cut out (1) 1/2" (13 mm) square and (4) 1 1/2" x 5/16" (4 cm x 8 mm) strips for the lid. Cut out (1) 1 1/4" (3 cm) square and (4) 1" x 1 1/4" (3 x 3 cm) squares for the box interior.

Coat the back of each piece of felt with craft glue and apply the pieces to the bottom and side wall interiors of the box and lid.

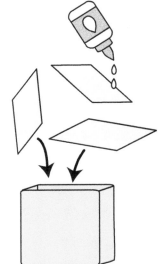

# PUPPY IN SQUARE GIFT BOX (continued)

To help place the felt pieces in the bottom of the box, invert the box and press the felt onto the floor of the box, then invert the box again so the felt piece will be in the correct position. Allow glue to dry completely.

## RIBBON

Cut and apply ribbon to box sides and box lid. For box, allow 1/2" (13 mm) of ribbon to fold over the top edge of the box and glue down. For box lid, glue and curl the ribbon under the lip of the lid. To make a bow, cut (8) 2" (5 cm) pieces of ribbon, (8) 1 1/2" (4 cm) pieces of ribbon, and (1) 1 3/4" (4 cm) piece. Apply a dab of glue to ribbon ends of the 2" and 1 1/2" (5 and 4 cm) pieces of ribbon, press ends tog, and allow loops to dry. Make 1 3/4" (4 cm) piece of ribbon into a loop and apply glue to overlapped ends.

With glued ends of the loops pointed toward the center of the box top, apply the 8 larger loops in a circle to the top of the box with the edges in the middle and glue or sew down. Glue or sew down the 8 smaller loops in a 2nd circle layered on top of larger loops. Glue the circle loop to the center of the bow.

## BOX HINGE

Tack down 2 corners of the box lid to the box to provide a "hinge" point.

## HEAD BOTTOM

With white yarn, make an 8-st adjustable ring.

**Rnd 1:** Sc 2 in each st around. (16 sts)

**Rnd 2:** Sc 2, sc 2 in next 2 sts, sc 2, ch 4, sk ch 4, sk 4, sc 2, sc 2 in next 2 sts, sc 2. (20 sts)

**Rnd 3:** Sc 8, sc in each ch of ch-4, sc 8. (20 sts)

**Rnd 4:** *Sc 4, sc2tog, sc 4; rep from * 1 more time. (18 sts)

**Rnd 5:** Sc 18.

**Rnd 6:** *Sc 1, sc2tog; rep from * 5 more times. (12 sts)

**Stuff head.**

**Rnd 7:** Sc2tog 6 times. (6 sts)

Fasten off and close hole.

## MUZZLE DETAIL

**Rnd 1:** Starting in lower right corner of muzzle opening, reattach white yarn, (sl st 1, ch 1, sc 1) in same st (counts as first sc). Cont to sc 9 sts around the inside of the muzzle opening. (10 sts)

**Rnd 2:** *Sc 2, sc2tog, sc1; rep from * 1 more time. (8 sts)

Fasten off, leaving a long tail.

Stuff muzzle, thread yarn tail through the fl of rnd 2, and pull to close hole. Use leftover yarn tail to patch any holes in the sides of the muzzle.

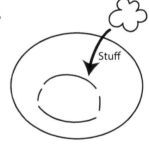

## HEAD TOP

With gray yarn, make an 8-st adjustable ring.

**Rnd 1:** Sc 2 in each st around. (16 sts)

**Rnd 2:** *Sc 1, sc 2 in next st; rep from * 7 more times. (24 sts)

**Rnd 3:** Sc 24.

**Rnd 4:** *Sc 1, sc2tog; rep from * 1 more time, hdc 2, sc 1, sl st 2, sc 1, ch 5, starting in 2nd ch from hook and working in back ridge loops, sl st 3, sc 1, cont working in rnd 3 sts, sc 1, sl st 2, sc 1, hdc 2, **sc2tog, sc 1; rep from ** 1 more time.

Place head top onto head bottom with ch-5 lined up with tip of the muzzle. Sew ch-5 down to the top and tip of muzzle, then sew the head top edge to head bottom.

Glue or sew on 4 mm plastic eyes. Using a single yarn ply from your black yarn or black embroidery thread, apply 1 short stitch above each eye for an eyebrow.

Using white yarn, sew back and forth through the head between the inner corners of the eye, pulling gently to sink the sides of the nose bridge.

# PUPPY IN SQUARE GIFT BOX (continued)

Cut (6) 3" (8 cm) pieces of white yarn. Using fringe knots, apply 3 strands to the edge of the cheeks. Trim short. Separate and soften yarn plies with fingers.

## NOSE

With black yarn, make a 3-st adjustable ring. Do not join ring. Cut yarn and pull yarn tail out through last st to secure.

With the rounded edge of the nose pointed down, sew nose to tip of muzzle (overlapping the end of the head top ch-6).

## EAR (MAKE 2)

With gray yarn, make a 5-st adjustable ring, ch 1, turn. Do not join ring. Work row in a semi-circle shape.

**Row 1:** Sl st 2, ch 2, hdc 1, ch 2, sl st in back ridge loop of 2nd ch from hook, ch 2, sl st 2.

**Fasten off.**

Sew flat edges of ears to the top of the head.

## BODY

With white yarn, make a 6-st adjustable ring.

**Rnd 1:** Sc 2 in each st around. (12 sts)

**Rnd 2:** *Sc 1, sc 2 in next st; rep from * 5 more times. (18 sts)

**Rnd 3:** Sc 18.

**Rnd 4:** *Sc 7, sc2tog; rep from * 1 more time. (16 sts)

**Rnd 5:** *Sc 6, sc2tog; rep from * 1 more time. (14 sts)

**Rnd 6:** *Sc 5, sc2tog; rep from * 1 more time. (12 sts)

**Rnd 7:** *Sc 1, sc2tog; rep from *

3 more times. (8 sts)

Fasten off yarn and stuff body. Leave neck edge open.

Sew open edge of neck to the bottom of the head.

## ARM AND PAW (MAKE 2)

With white yarn, ch 7.

**Rnd 1:** Starting in 2nd ch from hook and working in back ridge loops, sc 5, sc 3 back ridge loop of next ch. Rotate ch so front loops are facing up. Starting in next ch and working in front loops, sc 4, sc 2 in fl of next ch. (14 sts)

**Rnd 2:** Sc2tog 7 times. (7 sts)

**Rnd 3:** Sc 7.

Cut white yarn. Change to gray.

**Rnds 4–8:** Sc 7.

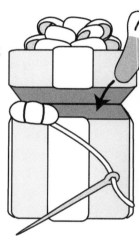

Using black embroidery floss, separate out 3 threads. Loop the 3-ply floss over the front of the paw slightly to the left and slightly to the right of center to define three toes. Drape the arm and paw over the front edge of the gift box and sew in place with the upper arm tucked inside the box.

Attach blue yarn to the bottom of the body. Draw the yarn up through the body and the top of the head. Attach the top of the head to the inner front edge of the box lid and then thread yarn down through the body and out through the bottom of the gift box. Secure yarn and weave in end.

Attach a jump ring to box lid directly above the head. Add hanger (page 18).

# KITTY IN ROUND GIFT BOX

····· DIFFICULTY: INTERMEDIATE * FINISHED SIZE: 3" TALL, 3" LONG (8 X 8 CM) ·······

## ⇌ MATERIALS ⇌

- Sock weight yarn in gray, pink, purple, tan, and white
- Hook size C (2.75 mm)
- Tapestry needle
- Black embroidery thread/floss
- Scissors
- 1/4" (6 mm) ribbon
- (2) 4 mm plastic eyes
- Polyester fiberfill
- 8" (20 cm) square of purple felt
- Craft glue or needle and thread
- (1) 8–10 mm jump ring
- Place marker

## BOX BASE

With purple yarn, make a 7-st adjustable ring.

**Rnd 1:** Sc 2 in each st around. (14 sts)

**Rnd 2:** *Sc 1, sc 2 in next st; rep from * 6 more times. (21 sts)

**Rnd 3:** *Sc 1, sc 2 in next st, sc 1; rep from * 6 more times. (28 sts)

**Rnd 4:** BPsc 28.

**Rnds 5–11:** Sc 28.

Fasten off.

## BOX LID

With purple yarn, make a 7-st adjustable ring.

**Rnd 1:** Sc 2 in each st around. (14 sts)

**Rnd 2:** *Sc 1, sc 2 in next st; rep from * 6 more times. (21 sts)

**Rnd 3:** *Sc 1, sc 2 in next st, sc 1; rep from * 6 more times. (28 sts)

**Rnd 4:** *Sc 2, sc 2 in next st, sc 1; rep from * 6 more times. (35 sts)

**Rnd 5:** BPsc 35.

**Rnds 6–7:** Sc 35.

Fasten off.

## FELT

From purple felt, cut out (1) 1/2" (13 mm) circle and (1) 5" x 5/16" (13 cm x 8 mm) strip for the lid (will trim as needed once fitted). Cut out (1) 1 1/4" (3 cm) circle and (4) 4" x 1" (10 x 3 cm) strips for the box interior.

Coat the back of each piece of felt with craft glue and apply the pieces to the bottom and side wall interiors of the box and lid.

# KITTY IN ROUND GIFT BOX (continued)

To help place the felt pieces in the bottom of the box, invert the box and press the felt onto the floor of the box, then invert the box again so the felt piece will be in the correct position. Allow glue to dry completely.

## RIBBON

Cut and apply ribbon to box sides and box top. For box, allow 1/2" (13 mm) of ribbon to fold over into the box and glue down. For box top, glue and curl the ribbon under the lip of the lid. To make a bow, cut (8) 2" (5 cm) pieces of ribbon, (8) 1 1/2" (4 cm) pieces of ribbon, and (1) 1 3/4" (4 cm) piece. Apply a dab of glue to ribbon ends of the 2" and 1 1/2" (5 and 4 cm) pieces of ribbon, press ends tog, and allow loops to dry. Make 1 3/4" (4 cm) piece of ribbon into a loop and apply glue to overlapped ends.

With glued ends of the loops pointed toward the center of the box top, apply the 8 larger loops in a circle to the top of the box with the edges in the middle and glue or sew

down. Glue or sew down the 8 smaller loops in a 2nd circle layered on top of larger loops. Glue the circle loop to the center of the bow.

## BOX HINGE

Tack down 2 sides of the box lid to the box to provide a "hinge" point.

## HEAD BOTTOM

With white yarn, make an 8-st adjustable ring.

**Rnd 1:** Sc 2 in each st around. (16 sts)

**Rnd 2:** Sc 2, sc 2 in next 2 sts, sc 8, sc 2 in next 2 sts, sc 2. (20 sts)

**Rnd 3:** Sc 8, ch 4, sk ch 4, sk 4, sc 8. (20 sts)

**Rnd 4:** Sc 8, sc in each ch of ch-4, sc 8. (20 sts)

**Rnd 5:** *Sc 4, sc2tog, sc 4; rep from * 1 more time. (18 sts)

**Rnd 6:** Sc 18.

**Rnd 7:** *Sc 1, sc2tog; rep from * 5 more times. (12 sts)

**Rnd 8:** Sc2tog 6 times. (6 sts)

Fasten off yarn and close hole.

## MUZZLE DETAIL

**Rnd 1:** Starting in lower right corner of muzzle opening, reattach white yarn (sl st 1, ch 1, sc 1) in same st (counts as first sc). Cont to sc 9 sts around the inside of the muzzle opening. (10 sts)

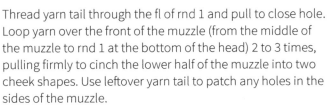
Pull

Fasten off, leaving a long tail for sewing.

Thread yarn tail through the fl of rnd 1 and pull to close hole. Loop yarn over the front of the muzzle (from the middle of the muzzle to rnd 1 at the bottom of the head) 2 to 3 times, pulling firmly to cinch the lower half of the muzzle into two cheek shapes. Use leftover yarn tail to patch any holes in the sides of the muzzle.

# KITTY IN ROUND GIFT BOX *(continued)*

## HEAD TOP

With tan yarn, make an 8-st adjustable ring.

**Rnd 1:** Sc 2 in each st around. (16 sts)

**Rnd 2:** *Sc 1, sc 2 in next st; rep from * 7 more times. (24 sts)

**Rnd 3:** Sc 24.

**Rnd 4:** Sc 1, sc2tog 2 times, hdc 1, dc 1, hdc 1, sc 1, sl st 2, sc 1, ch 3, starting in 2nd ch from hook and working in back ridge loops, sl st 1, sc 1, cont working in rnd 3 sts, sc 1, sl st 2, sc 1, hdc 1, dc 1, hdc1, sc2tog 2 times, sc 1.

Fasten off, leaving a long tail for sewing.

Place head top onto head bottom with ch-3 lined up with the muzzle. Sew ch-3 down to the face and tip of the muzzle, then sew the edge of head top down to head bottom.

Glue or sew on 4 mm plastic eyes. Using a single yarn ply of black yarn or black embroidery thread, apply 1 short stitch above each eye for an eyebrow.

Cut (6) 3" (8 cm) pieces of white yarn. Using fringe knots, apply 3 strands to the edge of the cheeks. Trim short. Separate and soften yarn plies with fingers.

## NOSE

Cut (1) 12" (31 cm) length of pink yarn and tie a square knot in the middle of the yarn. Draw the yarn tails through the face. The knot is positioned at the end of the kitty head top ch-3 detail.

Use 1-ply of black embroidery thread and embroider an upside-down Y shape directly under the nose for a mouth.

## EAR (MAKE 2)

With tan yarn, make a 5-st adjustable ring, ch 1, turn. Do not join ring. Work row in a semi-circle shape.

**Row 1:** Sl st 2, (sc 1, ch 2, sl st in back ridge loop of 2nd ch from hook, sc 1) in next st, sl st 2.

Fasten off.

Sew flat edges of ears to the top of the head.

## BODY

With white yarn, make a 6-st adjustable ring.

**Rnd 1:** Sc 2 in each st around. (12 sts)

**Rnd 2:** *Sc 1, sc 2 in next st; rep from * 5 more times. (18 sts)

**Rnd 3:** Sc 18.

**Rnd 4:** *Sc 7, sc2tog; rep from * 1 more time. (16 sts)

**Rnd 5:** *Sc 6, sc2tog; rep from * 1 more time. (14 sts)

**Rnd 6:** *Sc 5, sc2tog; rep from * 1 more time. (12 sts)

**Rnd 7:** *Sc 1, sc2tog; rep from * 3 more times. (8 sts)

Fasten off yarn and stuff body. Leave neck edge open.

Sew open edge of neck to the bottom of the head.

## ARM AND PAW (MAKE 2)

With white yarn, ch 7.

**Rnd 1:** Starting in 2nd ch from hook and working in back ridge loops, sc 5, sc 3 back ridge loop of next ch. Rotate ch so front loops are facing up. Starting in next ch and working in front loops, sc 4, sc 2 in fl of next ch. (14 sts)

**Rnd 2:** Sc2tog 7 times. (7 sts)

**Rnd 3:** Sc 7.

Cut white yarn. Change to tan.

**Rnds 4–8:** Sc 7. Fasten off.

Using black embroidery floss, separate out 3 threads. Drape the 3-ply floss over the front of the paw slightly to the left and slightly to the right of center to define three toes. Wrap the arm and paw over the front edge of the gift box and sew in place with the upper arm tucked inside the box.

Attach purple yarn to the bottom of the body. Draw the yarn up through the body and the top of the head. Attach the top of the head to the inner front edge of the box lid and then thread yarn down through the body and out through the bottom of the gift box. Secure yarn and weave in end.

Attach a jump ring to box lid directly above the head. Add hanger (page 18).

# ROCKING HORSE

······ DIFFICULTY: EASY * FINISHED SIZE: 3" TALL, 1 1/2" WIDE, 3" LONG (8 X 4 X 8 CM) ·······

## ⇌ MATERIALS ⇌

- Sock weight yarn in black, brown, and tan
- Hook size C (2.75 mm)
- Tapestry needle
- Scissors
- 8" (20 cm) square of stabilizer foam
- (2) 6/0 "E" gold seed beads
- Invisible thread
- Beading needle
- (1) 8–10 mm jump ring
- Place marker

## SEAT

With tan yarn, ch 30.

**Row 1:** Starting in 2nd ch from hook and working in back ridge loops, sc 29, ch 1, turn.

**Row 2:** Sk ch, sc 21, pm, sc 8 and fasten off, turn. (29 sts)

**Row 3:** (Sl st 1, ch 1, sc 1) in fl of marked st, in fl, sc 12, ch 1, turn. (13 sts)

**Rows 4–8:** Sk ch, sc 13, ch 1, turn. (13 sts)

**Row 9:** Sk ch, in fl, sc 13, ch 1, turn. (13 sts)

**Row 10:** Sk ch, sc 13, ch 1, turn. (13 sts)

**Row 11:** Sk ch, in fl, sc 13, ch 1, turn. (13 sts)

**Rows 12–16:** Sk ch, sc 13, ch 1, turn. (13 sts)

**Row 17:** Sk ch, in fl, sc 13, ch 1, turn. (13 sts)

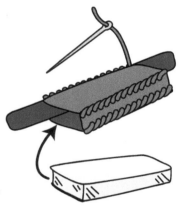

Cut (1) 2" x 1" (5 x 3 cm) rectangle of stabilizer foam. With the fl of rows 9, 11, and 17 facing out, sew the middle 13 sts of row 1 to the fl of row 17. Insert rectangle of foam into seat. Cover the short end of the seat with the extended ends of row 1, sewing the fl of the edge of row 1 to the open ends of the seat.

## NOSE (MAKE 2)

With tan yarn, ch 4, turn.

**Row 1:** Starting in 2nd ch from hook, sc 3, ch 1, turn. (3 sts)

**Row 2:** Sk ch, sc 2 in next st, sc 2, ch 1, turn. (4 sts)

**Row 3:** Sk ch, sc 4, ch 1, turn. (4 sts)

**Row 4:** Sk ch, (sc 1, pm, sc 1) in next st, pm, sc 3. (5 sts)

Fasten off and set aside.

# ROCKING HORSE *(continued)*

Hold head pieces tog so edges match up. With tan yarn, sc along the outer edges of the head, leaving the base open. Turn head inside out. Do not stuff. Sew the base of the neck to the top surface of the seat. The front edge of the neck should line up with the front edge of the seat.

## LEG (MAKE 4)

With tan yarn, ch 7.

**Row 1:** Starting in 2nd ch from hook and working in back ridge loops, sc 6, turn.

**Row 2:** Sk ch, sc 6, ch 1, turn. (6 sts)

**Row 3:** Sk ch, in fl, sc 6, ch 1, turn. (6 sts)

**Row 4:** Sk ch, sc 6, ch 1, turn. (6 sts)

**Row 5:** Sk ch, in fl, sc 6, ch 1, turn. (6 sts)

**Row 6:** Sk ch, sc 6, ch 1, turn. (6 sts)

**Row 7:** Sk ch, in fl, sc 19, ch 1, turn. (6 sts)

**Row 8:** Sk ch, sc 6. (6 sts)

Fasten off and cut yarn, leaving a long tail for sewing.

Cut (4) 3/8" x 3/4" (10 x 19 mm) strips of stabilizer foam. Place foam on WS of leg piece. With the fl of rows 3, 5, and 7 facing out, sew the edge of row 1 to the fl of row 8, enclosing the foam. Repeat on remaining legs.

Position and sew one open end of each leg to the bottom corners of the rocking horse seat.

## ROCKER (MAKE 2)

With tan yarn, ch 24.

**Row 1:** Starting in 2nd ch from hook and working in back ridge loops, sc 23, turn.

**Row 2:** Sk ch, sc 21, pm, sc 2 and fasten off, turn. (23 sts)

## HEAD (MAKE 2)

With tan yarn, ch 8, turn.

**Row 1:** Starting in 2nd ch from hook, sc 7, turn. (7 sts)

**Row 2:** Sk ch, sc 7, ch 1, turn. (7 sts)

**Row 3:** Sk ch, sc 5, sc2tog, ch 1, turn. (6 sts)

**Row 4:** Sk ch, sc 6, ch 1, turn. (6 sts)

**Row 5:** Sk ch, sc 4, sc2tog, ch 1, turn. (5 sts)

**Row 6:** Sk ch, sc 5. Starting with the marked st of nose row 4, sc 5 across nose, ch 1, turn. (10 sts)

**Row 7:** Sk ch, sc2tog, sc 6, sc2tog, ch 1, turn. (8 sts)

**Row 8:** Sk ch, sc2tog, sc 6, ch 1, turn. (7 sts)

**Row 9:** Sk ch, sc2tog, sc 3, sc2tog, ch 1, turn. (5 sts)

**Row 10:** Sk ch, sc2tog, sc 1, sc2tog. (3 sts)

Fasten off yarn, leaving a long tail for sewing.

**Row 3:** (Sl st 1, ch 1, sc 1) in fl of marked st, in fl, sc 18, ch 1, turn. (19 sts)

**Row 4:** Sk ch, sc 19, ch 1, turn. (19 sts)

**Row 5:** Sk ch, in fl, sc 19, ch 1, turn. (19 sts)

**Row 6:** Sk ch, sc 19, ch 1, turn. (19 sts)

**Row 7:** Sk ch, in fl, sc 19, ch 1, turn. (19 sts)

**Row 8:** Sk ch, sc 19. (19 sts)

Fasten off, leaving a long tail for sewing.

Cut (1) 3/8" x 3" (10 mm x 8 cm) stripe of stabilizer foam. Place foam on WS of rocker piece. With the fl of rows 3, 5, and 7 facing out, sew the edge of the middle 19 sts of row 1 to the fl of row 8, enclosing the foam. Fold the extended ends of rows 1 and 2 over the open ends of the rocker and sew matching edges tog.

Sew the open edges of the legs to the top of the rockers, leaving about 10 to 11 rows of space between the front and back legs.

## EAR (MAKE 2)

With tan yarn, make a 4-st adjustable ring.

**Rnd 1:** Sl st 2, (sl st 1, ch 2, sl st in 2nd ch from hook, sl st 1) in next st, sl st 1.

Fasten off in next st and cut yarn, leaving a long tail for sewing.

Attach round end of ears to sides of the head.

## MANE AND TAIL

Cut (14 to 16) 8" (20 cm) pieces of brown yarn. Hold a pair of strands tog and, starting at the top of the head, between the ears, attach double strands to the head using a fringe knot. Cont to attach yarn down the back of neck. Trim to desired length.

Cut (5 to 6) 10" (25 cm) pieces of brown yarn and hold strands tog in a bundle. Attach center of yarn bundle to back of seat using a fringe knot and trim tail to desired length.

## BRIDLE

With black yarn, ch 10. Fasten off, leaving a long tail for sewing. Wrap bridle around horse nose, sew in place, and weave in ends.

With invisible thread and a beading needle, sew a gold seed bead on either side of the bridle.

Sew on a jump ring to the back of the neck. Add a hanger (page 18).

IF THE TAIL AND MANE AREN'T STAYING FLAT ENOUGH, TRY APPLYING A SMALL AMOUNT OF HAIR GEL TO THE YARN WITH YOUR FINGERTIPS TO STYLE AND SMOOTH.

# RAG DOLL

······ DIFFICULTY: EASY * FINISHED SIZE: 3 1/2" TALL, 1 3/4" WIDE (9 X 4 CM) ······

## ⇟ MATERIALS ⇟

- Sock weight yarn in:
  Skin colors: brown, ivory, or tan*
  Hair colors: black, red,* or yellow
  Dress colors: blue,* green, or red
- Apron: white
- Hook size C (2.75 mm)
- Embroidery floss in black and dark pink
- Pink felt
- 1/4" (6 mm) hole punch
- Cuticle scissors
- Sewing needle
- Tapestry needle
- Scissors
- (1) 8–10 mm jump ring
- Place marker
  *Yarn colors used as shown.

## ARMS

With skin-color yarn, ch 16.

**Row 1:** Starting in 2nd ch from hook and working in back ridge loops, hdc 2, sc 11, hdc 2, ch 1, turn. (15 sts)

**Row 2:** Sk ch, hdc 2, sc 11, hdc 2, ch 1, turn. (15 sts)

**Row 3:** Sk ch, hdc 2, sc 11, hdc 2, turn. (15 sts)

Fasten off, leaving a long tail for sewing. Fold piece in half the long way and match up edges. Sew long edges tog.

## LEGS

With skin-color yarn, ch 20.

**Row 1:** Starting in 2nd ch from hook and working in back ridge loops, hdc 2, sc 15, hdc 2, ch 1, turn. (19 sts)

**Row 2:** Sk ch, hdc 2, sc 15, hdc 2, ch 1, turn. (19 sts)

**Row 3:** Sk ch, hdc 2, sc 15, hdc 2, turn. (19 sts)

Fasten off, leaving a long tail for sewing. Fold piece in half the long way and match up edges. Sew long edges tog.

## HEAD AND BODY (MAKE 2)

### Head

With skin-color yarn, make a 6-st adjustable ring.

**Rnd 1:** Sc 2 in each st around. (12 sts)

**Rnd 2:** *Sc 1, sc 2 in next st; rep from * 5 more times. (18 sts)

**Rnd 3:** *Sc 2, sc 2 in next st; rep from * 5 more times. (24 sts)

**Rnd 4:** *Sc 1, sc 2 in next st, sc 2; rep from * 5 more times. (30 sts)

### Body

Sl st in next st and ch 5.

**Row 1:** Working in back ridge loops, sc 3 in 2nd ch from hook, sc in back ridge loops of next 3 ch, sc in st at the base

# RAG DOLL (continued)

st of ch-5, sl st 1 in next st of rnd 4 of head, ch 1, turn. (7 sts)

**Row 2:** Sk ch 1, sk sl st 1, sc 4, sc 2 in next 3 sts. Starting in next ch and working in front loops of ch-5, sc 4, sl st in rnd 4 of head. (14 sts)

Fasten off, leaving a long tail for sewing.

Place body/head pieces WS tog with just the middle portions of the leg and arm pieces sandwiched between them. Whip stitch around edge of body, securing the leg and arm pieces sticking out along the edges as you close the body/head seam. Add a small amount of stuffing to head before closing seam.

Stuff

## DRESS

With dress-color yarn, ch 12, sl st in first ch to make a loop, taking care not to twist the ch.

**Rnd 1:** Working in back ridge loops and starting in 2nd ch from hook, sc 12.

**Rnd 2:** Sc 3, ch 3, sk ch-3, sk 3, sc 3, ch 3, sk ch-3, sk 3. (12 sts)

**Rnd 3:** Sc 3, sc in each ch of ch-3, sc 3, sc in each ch of ch-3. (12 sts)

**Rnds 4–5:** Sc 12.

**Rnd 6:** *Sc 2, sc 2 in next st; rep from * 3 more times. (16 sts)

**Rnd 7:** *Sc 2, sc 2 in next st, sc 1; rep from * 3 more times. (20 sts)

**Rnd 8:** *Sc 2, sc 2 in next st, sc 2; rep from *3 times. (24 sts)

Fasten off. Weave in end.

Slip dress onto body with arms threaded through the sleeve holes.

## APRON

With white yarn, ch 7.

**Row 1:** Working in back ridge loops and starting in 2nd ch from hook, sc 6, ch 1, turn.

**Row 2:** Sk ch, sc 6, ch 1, turn. (6 sts)

**Row 3:** Sk ch, sc2tog, sc 2, sc2tog, ch 1, turn. (4 sts)

**Rows 4–5:** Sk ch, sc 4, ch 1, turn. (4 sts)

**Row 6:** Sk ch, sc 4. (4 sts) Do not cut.

**Cont to strap and apron edge details.**

## STRAP AND APRON EDGE DETAILS

Ch 10, starting in 2nd ch from hook, (sl st 1, ch 2, sl st 1) in back ridge loop of each ch, sl st 6 down the side of the apron toward row 1, (sl st 1, ch 2, sl st 1) in each st across the bottom of row 1, sl st 4 up the other side of the apron toward the end of row 6.

In the first st of row 6, ch 10, starting in 2nd ch from hook, (sl st 1, ch 2, sl st 1) in back ridge loop of each ch.

Fasten off, leaving a long tail for sewing.

Wrap straps over shoulders, cross at the back, and connect to the sides of the apron, taking care not to twist the straps as you work. Sew in place with white yarn and weave in ends.

Back

## HAIR OPTIONS

### Straight hair

Double up hair-colored yarn on tapestry needle and gently apply long stitches to the head from the center part to the sides. Repeat until top and back of head is covered. Cut (8) 6" (15 cm) pieces of hair-colored yarn and separate into (2) 4-piece bundles. Attach bundles to sides of head with a fringe knot and trim to desired length.

### Curly hair

**With hair-colored yarn and working into a surface sp or st:** *(ch 3, sk 2, sc 1, sl st 1) in next surface sp or st; rep from * in next sp or st on the head until the whole head surface is filled with tight curls.

### Fringe hair

Cut hair-colored yarn into 4" to 5" (10 to 13 cm) pieces and attach to head with fringe knots. Separate yarn plies and brush out with a nit comb. Style or trim as desired.

## FACE

Cut (1) 12" (31 cm) length of embroidery floss in black and separate it into (2) 3-ply strands. Using a 3-ply strand and embroidery needle, embroider closed eyes and mouth onto front of head.

Using pink felt, use a hole punch to cut out two small circles. Use a pair of cuticle scissors to cut out (1) 1/2" (13 mm)-wide heart. Glue the circles to the face at the corners of the mouth. Apply a small dot of glue to the back of the heart and attach to the front of the apron.

Cut (1) 12" (31 cm) length of embroidery floss in dark pink and separate it into (2) 3-ply strands. Using a 3-ply strand and embroidery needle, embroider a small running stitch around the inside edge of the heart.

Sew on a jump ring. Add a hanger (page 18).

# SOCKS

······ DIFFICULTY: EASY * FINISHED SIZE: 3 1/4" TALL, 2 1/2" WIDE (8 X 6 CM) ······

## ⇌ MATERIALS ⇌

- Sock weight yarn in green and red
- Hook size C (2.75 mm)
- Tapestry needle
- Scissors
- Polyester fiberfill
- (1) 8–10 mm jump ring
- Place marker

## SOCK (MAKE 2)

With green yarn, make a 4-st adjustable ring.

**Rnd 1:** Sc 2 in each st around. (8 sts)

**Rnds 2–3:** Sc 8.

**Rnd 4:** *Sc 1, sc 2 in next st; rep from * 3 more times. (12 sts)

**Rnd 5:** *Sc 1, sc 2 in next st; rep from * 5 more times. (18 sts)

**Rnds 6–7:** Sc 18.

**Drop green yarn. Change to red. (On rnd 10, substitute green for red.)**

**Rnd 8:** *Sc 7, sc2tog; rep from * 1 more time. (16 sts)

**Rnds 9–11:** Sc 16.

**Row 12:** Sc 16, drop red, change to green, ch 1, turn.

**Row 13:** Sk ch, sc 8, ch 1, turn, leaving rem sts unworked. (8 sts)

**Rows 14–16:** Sk ch, sc 8, ch 1, turn. (8 sts)

**Row 17:** Sk ch, *sc 1, sc2tog, sc 1; rep from * 1 more time, ch 1, turn. (6 sts)

**Row 18:** Sk ch, sc2tog, sc 2, sc2tog, ch 1, turn. (4 sts)

**Row 19:** Sk ch, sc2tog 2 times, ch 1, turn. (2 sts)

**Rnd 20:** Sk ch, sc 2, pick up 4 sc sts along the green edge, sc 8 in unworked sts from row 13, pick up 4 sc sts along the green edge. (18 sts)

**Change to red yarn. (On rnds 23, 26, 29 and 32, substitute green for red.)**

**Rnds 21–32:** Sc 18.

Fasten off and weave in end.

Overlap socks and attach with a few sts to hold the overlap in place.

Sew on a jump ring. Add a hanger (page 18).

# LUMP OF COAL

······ DIFFICULTY: BEGINNER * FINISHED SIZE: 1 1/4" TALL, 1 1/4" WIDE (3 X 3 CM) ······

## ⇌ MATERIALS ⇌

- Sock weight yarn in black
- Hook size C (2.75 mm)
- Tapestry needle
- Scissors
- Polyester fiberfill
- (1) 8–10 mm jump ring
- Place marker

## COAL

With black yarn, make an 8-st adjustable ring.

**Rnd 1:** Sc 2 in each st around. (16 sts)

**Rnd 2:** *Sc 3, sc 2 in next st; rep from * 3 more times. (20 sts)

**Rnd 3:** *Sc 4, sc 2 in next st; rep from * 3 more times. (24 sts)

**Rnd 4:** *Sc 5, sc 2 in next st; rep from * 3 more times. (28 sts)

**Rnds 5–9:** Sc 28.

**Rnd 10:** *Sc 5, sc2tog; rep from * 3 more times. (24 sts)

**Rnd 11:** *Sc 4, sc2tog; rep from * 3 more times. (20 sts)

**Rnd 12:** *Sc 3, sc2tog; rep from * 3 more times. (16 sts)

**Stuff 50% full.**

**Rnd 13:** Sc2tog 8 times. (8 sts)

Fasten off, leaving a 20" (51 cm) tail. Close hole.

Using leftover yarn tail, sew through the surface of the coal at random points to create divots and bumps. Sharper edge details can be created by pinching the surface to create a small lip and running black yarn through the pinched surface to hold the shaping.

Once happy with the lumpiness of your coal, attach jump ring. Fasten off, and weave in end.

Sew on a jump ring. Add a hanger (page 18).

# DECK THE HALLS

Nothing heralds the arrival of the holidays quite like festive decorations! Twinkling lights, shiny sleigh bells, lush green wreaths, and the warm glow of candles help to set the stage for the season. This lovely collection of festive decor is perfect for adding a bit of Christmas charm to any place in need of some holiday cheer.

# TREE LIGHTS

······ DIFFICULTY: EASY * FINISHED SIZE: 3" TALL, 1 1/4" WIDE (8 X 3 CM) ······

## ⇌ MATERIALS ⇌

- Sock weight yarn in blue, dark green, red, white, and yellow
- Hook size C (2.75 mm)
- Tapestry needle
- Scissors
- Polyester fiberfill
- (1) 8–10 mm jump ring
- Place marker

## SOCKET

With dark green, make a 6-st adjustable ring.

**Base Rnd:** Sc 2 in each st around. (12 sts)

**Row 1:** Ch 5, starting in 2nd ch from hook and working in back ridge loops, sc 4, BPsc in next st of base rnd, turn. (5 sts)

**Row 2:** Sk 1, in bl, sl st 4, ch 1, turn. (4 sts)

**Row 3:** Sk ch, work in the unworked loops at the base of the sl st 4 (the loops will be in the back of your work, behind the ridge of slip stitches), sc into these 4 bls, BPsc in next st of the base rnd, turn. (5 sts)

Repeat rows 2–3 until you have worked 12 BPsc sts into the base rnd. BPslst in last stitch of base rnd. Fasten off, leaving a long tail for sewing. Sew up the side seam of the light base.

## BULB

With blue, yellow, or red, make a 6-st adjustable ring. (You will make 1 of each color.)

**Rnd 1:** Sc 2 in each st around. (12 sts)

**Rnds 2–4:** Sc 12.

**Rnd 5:** Sc 2 in each st around. (24 sts)

**Rnd 6:** *Sc 5, sc 2 in next st; rep from * 3 more times. (28 sts)

**Rnds 7–8:** Sc 28.

**Rnd 9:** *Sc2tog, sc 5; rep from * 3 more times. (24 sts)

**Rnd 10:** Sc 24.

**Rnd 11:** *Sc 4, sc2tog; rep from * 3 more times. (20 sts)

**Rnd 12:** Sc 20.

**Rnd 13:** *Sc2tog, sc 3; rep from * 3 more times. (16 sts)

**Rnd 14:** Sc 16.

**Rnd 15:** *Sc 2, Sc2tog; rep from * 3 more times. (12 sts)

**Rnd 16:** Sc 12.

**Stuff.**

**Rnd 17:** *Sc2tog, sc 1; rep from * 3 more times. (8 sts)

**Rnd 18:** *Sc 2, sc2tog; rep from * 1 more time. (6 sts)

Fasten off and weave yarn tail into remaining 6 sts. Pull tightly to close hole.

Place the socket over the bottom of the bulb (rnds 1–4) and sew in place with a few stitches.

## WIRE (MAKE 2)

Make (2) 2" (5 cm) twisted cords of dark green yarn for wire. Cut 20" (51 cm) of dark green yarn and tie the ends tog with a square knot to make a large loop. Hook finger through the end of the yarn loop and spin your finger around to twist the yarn tog. Once twisted tightly, the yarn will start to twist over on itself when you give the loop some slack. Tie the ends of the twisted cord tog to hold the twist and pull the knot through the side of the light bulb base, allowing the wire to stick out on the side. Repeat on the other side of the light bulb base.

You can also attach the lights to each other with twisted cords between them.

## REFLECTION DETAIL

Using white yarn, embroider a large teardrop shape and small group of 2 to 3 satin stitches to the side of the light for a reflection detail. Repeat on each light bulb.

Sew on a jump ring. Add a hanger (page 18).

# RINGING BELL

······ DIFFICULTY: EASY * FINISHED SIZE: 1 3/4" TALL, 1 1/2" WIDE (4 X 4 CM) ······

## ⇌ MATERIALS ⇌

- Sock weight yarn in green and light yellow
- (1) 1 1/2" (4 cm) plastic cabone ring
- Invisible thread
- (1) 11/0 silver seed bead
- (1) 3/8" (10 mm) drop pearl bead
- (3) 6/0 "E" red seed beads
- Hook size C (2.75 mm)
- Beading needle
- Scissors
- (1) 8–10 mm jump ring
- Place marker

## BELL BODY

With light yellow, make a sl st knot on your hook.

**Rnd 1:** Sc 40 around the edge of (1) 1 1/2" (4 cm) plastic cabone ring, encasing the ring in the sc sts.

**Rnd 2:** Orient the stitches so they run along the top surface of the ring, sc2tog 20 times. (20 sts)

**Rnds 3–6:** Sc 20.

**Rnd 7:** FPsc 20.

**Rnd 8:** Working in the rnd 6 sts directly behind the rnd 7 FPsc sts, sc 20. (20 sts)

**Rnd 9:** *Sc 3, sc2tog; rep from * 3 more times. (16 sts)

**Rnd 10:** *Sc2tog, sc 2; rep from * 3 more times. (12 sts)

**Rnd 11:** Sc2tog 6 times. (6 sts)

Fasten off, leaving a long tail for sewing. Wind yarn tail through remaining stitches and pull gently to close hole.

## CLAPPER

Cut (1) 12" (31 cm) length of invisible thread and double it up (creating a loop). Thread a silver seed bead onto the ends of the doubled-up thread, then draw the ends of the thread through the thread loop to secure the bead (like a fringe knot). Draw the needle through the drop pearl bead (stacking it on top of the silver seed bead). Draw the needle out through the top of the bell. Adjust the height of the pearl bead and secure the thread. Weave in end. Sew a jump ring to top of bell. Add a hanger (page 18).

## HOLLY LEAF (MAKE 2)

With green, ch 6, sl st in first st of ch to make a loop, ch 1.

**Rnd 1:** Working in ch-6 sp, *sl st 1, ch 2, sl st in base of ch 2; rep from * 6 more times.

Sl st to fasten off yarn in ch-6 sp and cut yarn, leaving a long tail. Use leftover yarn tail to close and sew up the seam in the middle of the leaf.

Attach leaves to bell top. With invisible thread and a beading needle, attach 3 red beads at the base of the leaves.

# SLEIGH BELL

······ DIFFICULTY: EASY * FINISHED SIZE: 2" TALL, 2" WIDE (5 X 5 CM) ······

## ≑ MATERIALS ≑

- Sock weight yarn in black, gray, and white
- (1) 1 3/4" (4 cm)-diameter plastic cat toy ball with bell or polyester fiberfill
- Hook size C (2.75 mm)
- Tapestry needle
- Scissors
- (1) 8–10 mm jump ring
- Place marker

## BELL HALVES (MAKE 2)

With gray yarn, make an 8-st adjustable ring.

**Rnd 1:** Sc 2 in each st around. (16 sts)

**Rnd 2:** *Sc 3, sc 2 in next st; rep from * 3 more times. (20 sts)

**Rnd 3:** *Sc 2, sc 2 in next st, sc 2; rep from * 3 more times. (24 sts)

**Rnd 4:** *Sc 1, sc 2 in next st, sc 4; rep from * 3 more times. (28 sts)

**Rnd 5:** *Sc 3, sc 2 in next st, sc 3; rep from * 3 more times. (32 sts)

**Rnd 6:** *Sc 2, sc 2 in next st, sc 5; rep from * 3 more times. (36 sts)

**Rnds 7–8:** Sc 36.

**Rnd 9:** FPsc 36.

Fasten off, leaving a long tail for sewing. Sleigh bell halves should reach halfway up the side of the plastic cat toy bell ball. If your cat toy runs small, you can skip rnd 6 or rnds 5 and 6 before crocheting 2 rnds without an inc plus the FPsc rnd for a better fit.

Enclose the toy between the two bell halves. Pair up the rnd 9 rnds, (sl st, ch 1) through the first pair of FPsc sts. Cont to sl st through each pair of sts all the way around. Fasten off and weave in end. If you do not wish to use a plastic cat ball toy, stuff the bell as you close the seam around the middle.

## BELL OPENING

With black yarn, make a 4-st adjustable ring.

**Rnd 1:** *Sc 1, ch 5, working in back ridge loops and starting in 2nd ch from hook, sc 2 in next ch, sl st 3; rep from * 3 more times.

**Cut black yarn. Change to gray.**

**Rnd 2:** Working in bl, *sl st 4, sl st 2 in next 3 sts at the top of the ch, sl st 3; rep from * 3 more times.

## ASSEMBLY

Sew bell opening onto the bottom half of the sleigh bell. Using white yarn, embroider a large teardrop shape and small group of 2 to 3 satin stitches to the side of the upper half of the bell for a reflection detail. Sew on a jump ring. Add a hanger (page 18).

# WREATH

DIFFICULTY: INTERMEDIATE * FINISHED SIZE: 2 3/4" TALL, 2 3/4" WIDE (7 X 7 CM)

## ⇌ MATERIALS ⇌

- Sock weight yarn in brown, dark green, medium green, and purple
- Hook size E (3.5 mm) for the wreath
- Hook size C (2.75 mm) for the other parts
- (1) 2" (5 cm) wooden cabone ring
- Tapestry needle
- Sewing needle
- Invisible thread
- (12) Pearl beads
- Scissors
- Polyester fiberfill
- (1) 8–10 mm jump ring
- Place marker

## WREATH

Hold dark and medium green yarn strands tog as you work.

Place a slip knot onto size E hook. Holding the yarn strands tog, sc 30 around the wooden cabone ring, encasing the ring in the sc sts, ch 1, turn. (30 sts)

**Row 1:** Sk ch, *FPsc, ch 2, sl st in FPsc st; rep from * 29 more times, ch 1, turn.

**Row 2:** Sk ch, working in the front and back loops directly above the FPsc sts, sc 30, ch 1, turn.

**Row 3:** Sk ch, *FPsc, ch 2, sl st in FPsc st, FPslst; rep from * 14 more times, ch 1, turn.

**Row 4:** Sk ch, working in the front and back loops directly above the FPsc sts, sc 30, ch 1, turn.

**Row 5:** Sk ch, *FPsc, ch 2, sl st in FPsc st; rep from * 29 more times, ch 1, turn.

**Row 6:** Sk ch, working in the front and back loops directly above the FPsc sts, sc 30, ch 1, turn.

**Row 7:** Sk ch, *FPsc, ch 2, sl st in FPsc st, sk next st; rep from * 14 more times, ch 1, turn.

**Row 8:** Sk ch, working in the front and back loops directly above the FPsc sts, ch 1, sc2tog 15 times. (15 sts)

Fasten off, leaving a long tail for sewing.

Working along the inside edge of the ring, sew row 8 to row 1 in the following manner: match up 1 st from the edge of row 8 with 2 sts at the base of row 1 and sew tog. Pull tightly as you sew to curl row 8 and row 1 tog (enclosing the wooden ring underneath). Fasten off and weave in ends.

## BOW

With purple yarn and the size C hook, ch 20 and join last ch to first ch with a sl st to form a ring.

**Rnds 1–3:** Sc 20.

**Rnd 4:** Sc2tog 10 times. (10 sts)

**Rnd 5:** Sc 2 in each st around. (20 sts)

**Rnds 6–8:** Sc 20.

Fasten off, leaving a long tail for sewing.

## BOW TAIL

With purple yarn, ch 31.

**Row 1:** Starting in 2nd ch from hook and working in back ridge loops, sc 30, ch 1, turn. (30 sts)

**Row 2:** Sk ch, sc 30, ch 1, turn. (30 sts)

**Row 3:** Sk ch, sl st 30. (30 sts)

Fasten off.

Flatten bow piece so that rnds 1 and 8 are oriented at the top and bottom of the work. Wrap yarn tail tightly around the center to shape the two sides of the bow. Sew the middle of bow tail to back of bow, allowing the tails to hang down.

## PINECONE (MAKE 3)

With brown yarn and the size C hook, make a 4-st adjustable ring.

**Rnd 1:** In bl, *sc 1, sc 2 in next st; rep from * 1 more time. (6 sts)

**Rnd 2:** In bl, sc 6.

**Rnd 3:** In bl, *sc 1, sc 2 in next st; rep from * 2 more times. (9 sts)

**Rnds 4–5:** In bl, sc 9.

Lightly stuff.

Fasten off, leaving a long tail for sewing. Wind yarn tail through remaining 9 sts and pull gently to close hole.

Position and attach pinecones to the front of the wreath.

With needle and invisible thread, attach 4 groupings of white pearl beads in clusters of three between the pinecones.

Sew on a jump ring. Add a hanger (page 18).

# CANDLE

## ⇋ MATERIALS ⇋

- Sock weight yarn in black, light yellow, orange, red-orange, white, and yellow
- Hook size C (2.75 mm)
- (1) 1 1/2" (4 cm) plastic cabone ring
- (1) 1 3/4" (4 cm) double-prong hair clip
- Tapestry needle
- Scissors
- Polyester fiberfill
- Place marker

## CANDLE

With white, make a 5-st adjustable ring.

**Rnd 1:** Sc 2 in each st around. (10 sts)

**Rnd 2:** BPsc 10.

**Rnds 3–17:** Sc 10.

**Rnd 18:** Sl st 2, sc 2, hdc 2, sc 2, sl st 2. (10 sts)

Fasten off and weave in ends.

Stuff candle (using back of crochet hook to push in stuffing if needed).

## WAX DRIP

With white, make a 6-st adjustable ring.

**Rnd 1:** Sc 2 in each st around. (12 sts)

**Rnd 2:** BPsc 12.

For the drip details, randomly alternate between chs of 3, 4, 5, or 6.

**Rnd 3:** *Sl st 1, ch 3/4/5/6, sc 2 in back ridge loop of 2nd ch from hook, sl st in remaining back ridge loops as well as the base of ch, sl st 1; rep from * 5 more times.

Sew rnd 2 of wax drip to rnd 18 of candle. Tack down the wax drips to the sides of the candle. Draw yarn through the top of the wax drip down to the base of the candle and pull gently to sink the center of the wax drip down slightly.

## CANDLE HOLDER DISH

With yellow, make a 5-st adjustable ring.

**Rnd 1:** Sc 2 in each st around. (10 sts)

**Rnd 2:** *Sc 1, sc 2 in next st; rep from * 4 more times. (15 sts)

**Rnd 3:** *Sc 1, sc 2 in next st, sc 1; rep from * 4 more times. (20 sts)

**Rnd 4:** Place plastic cabone ring in front of work, insert hook through ring and work 2 st in each st around (enclosing the ring inside the sc sts). (40 sts)

**Rnd 5:** Sc 40.

Sl st to fasten off yarn in next st. Weave in ends.

## CANDLE BASE

With yellow, make a 6-st adjustable ring.

**Rnd 1:** Sc 2 in each st around. (12 sts)

**Rnds 2–5:** Sc 12.

**Rnd 6:** Loosely FPsc 12.

Fasten off, leaving a long tail for sewing.

Insert candle into candle base. Run a few stitches through the bottom of both pieces to secure.

Attach candle base to WS of candle holder dish. RS of candle holder dish should be facing down.

## HANDLE

With yellow, ch 21.

**Row 1:** Working in back ridge loops of ch and starting in 2nd ch from hook, sc 20, ch 1, turn. (20 sts)

**Row 2:** Sk ch, sc 20.

Fasten off, leaving long tail for sewing.

Fold handle in half so short ends match up. Sew short ends tog to make a teardrop-shaped loop. Place sewn ends into space between the candle base and the inside edge of the candle holder dish. Sew candle holder handle to candle holder dish.

## FLAME

With light yellow yarn, make a 5-st adjustable ring.

**Rnd 1:** Sc 2, (sc 1, ch 2, sc 1) in next st, sc 2. Cut light yellow, change to orange, ch 1, turn. (6 sts)

**Row 2:** Sk ch, sc 3, (sc 1, ch 2, sc 1) in ch-2 sp, sc 3. Cut orange, change to red-orange, ch 1, turn. (8 sts)

**Row 3:** Sk ch, sc 4, (sc 1, ch 2, sc 1) in ch-2 sp, sc 4, turn. (10 sts)

Cut red-orange, leaving a long tail for sewing.

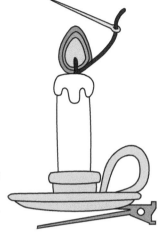

Thread red-orange yarn tail and sew back and forth between the first and last red-orange sts on row 3, pulling tightly as you sew to cinch the bottom of the flame tog. Fasten off red-orange yarn tail to secure shaping.

Draw all leftover flame yarn tails down through the top of the candle to hide them. Using black yarn and a tapestry needle, attach black yarn to the middle of the candle top and then draw through the middle of the flame and back to the candle top in a loop motion 2 to 3 times. This creates a wick detail and secures the flame to the top of the candle.

Holding the double-prong hair clip with the flat side against the bottom of the completed candle holder dish, insert the prongs through the bottom surface of the candle holder dish. The fit should be fairly tight without glue, but feel free to apply a thin coat of craft glue to the prongs being inserted into the work for a more secure hold if you prefer. This allows the ornament to be clipped onto a branch of your Christmas tree.

# PEPPERMINT PALS

These three fuzzy friends have a sweet tooth! Fortunately, there are plenty of tasty treats to go around during the holidays. Rabbit, Hedgehog, and Squirrel will each make a cute addition to any holiday ornament collection as they enjoy their peppermint candies.

# HEDGEHOG

## ⇒ MATERIALS ⇐

- Sock weight yarn in brown, red, tan, and white
- Hook size C (2.75 mm)
- (3) 4 mm plastic eyes
- Craft glue
- Black embroidery floss
- Tapestry needle
- Scissors
- Polyester fiberfill
- (1) 8–10 mm jump ring
- Place marker

## HEAD

With tan yarn, ch 4.

**Rnd 1:** Starting in 2nd ch from hook and working in back ridge loops, sc 2, sc 5 in back ridge loop of next ch. Rotate ch so front loops are facing up. Starting in next st and working in front loops, sc 1, sc 4 in fl of next ch. (12 sts)

**Rnd 2:** Sc 2 in next st, sc 1, sc 2 in next 5 sts, sc 1, sc 2 in next 4 sts. (22 sts)

**Rnd 3:** Sc 2, ch 2, sk ch-2, sk 2, sc 18. (22 sts)

**Rnd 4:** *Sc 7, sc2tog, sc 2; rep from * 1 more time. (20 sts)

**Rnd 5:** Sc 20.

**Rnd 6:** *Sc 2, sc2tog; rep from * 4 more times. (15 sts)

**Rnd 7:** Sc 15.

**Rnd 8:** *Sc 1, sc2tog; rep from * 4 more times. (10 sts)

**Rnd 9:** Sc 10.

Fasten off and stuff head. Close seam at the bottom of the head with a mattress stitch.

## MUZZLE DETAIL

**Rnd 1:** Starting in lower right corner of muzzle opening, reattach tan yarn (sl st 1, ch 1, sc 1) in same st (counts as first st). Cont to sc 7 more sts around the inside of the muzzle opening. (8 sts)

Fasten off in next st, leaving a long tail for sewing.

Pull

Thread yarn tail through the fl of rnd 1 and pull to close hole. Weave in yarn tail.

Take (1) 12" (31 cm) length of yarn and fasten it to the middle of rnd 1 at the bottom of the head. Draw the yarn up and out through the front of the head at rnd 4, slightly to the right of the muzzle. Reinsert needle slightly to the left of the muzzle at rnd 4 and draw out at the bottom of the head, pulling firmly to sink the bridge of the nose down into the head. Tie the yarn tails tog and weave knot and tails into the head.

# HEDGEHOG (continued)

## FACE

Cover the stems of the plastic eyes with a bit of craft glue and insert into the middle of the muzzle (to be the nose) and above the muzzle with 3 sts of space between them (to be the eyes).

With 3-strand black embroidery floss, embroider an upside-down Y under the nose, and a line over each eye for an eyebrow.

## EAR (MAKE 2)

With tan, make a 4-st adjustable ring and fasten off in center of ring.

Sew flat edge of ears to upper half of head.

## BODY

With tan yarn, make a 6-st adjustable ring.

**Rnd 1:** Sc 2 in each sc around. (12 sts)

**Rnd 2:** *Sc 2, sc 2 in next sc; rep from * 3 more times. (16 sts)

**Rnd 3:** *Sc 3, sc 2 in next sc; rep from * 3 more times. (20 sts)

**Rnd 4:** *Sc 4, sc 2 in next sc; rep from * 3 more times. (24 sts)

**Rnd 5:** *Sc 4, sc2tog; rep from * 3 more times. (20 sts)

**Rnd 6:** Sc 20.

**Rnd 7:** *Sc 3, sc2tog; rep from * 3 more times. (16 sts)

**Rnds 8–9:** Sc 16.

**Rnd 10:** *Sc 2, sc2tog; rep from * 3 more times. (12 sts)

**Rnd 11:** Sc 12.

Stuff 50% full. Fasten off, leaving a long tail for sewing.

Flatten and sew rnd 11 of body closed. Sew to lower back of head (between rnds 2 and 3), allowing head to flop over the chest slightly. Sew bottom of chin to front of body to hold pose in place.

## PAW (MAKE 4)

With tan yarn, ch 4.

**Rnd 1:** Starting in 2nd ch from hook and working in back ridge loops, sc 2, sc 4 in next st. Rotate ch so front loops are facing up. Starting in next ch and working in front loops, sc 1, sc 3 in next st. (10 sts)

**Rnd 2:** Sc 10.

**Rnd 3:** Sc 3, sc2tog, sc 3, sc2tog. (8 sts)

**Rnds 4–5:** Sc 8.

**Rnd 6:** Sc 2, sc2tog, sc 2, sc2tog. (6 sts)

Lightly stuff.

**Rnd 7:** Sc 6.

Fasten off and weave yarn through remaining sts. Pull tightly to close hole.

For the feet, use leftover yarn tails to attach the top surface of two paws to bottom of the body with the larger ends facing up. For the hands, sew the smaller ends of the remaining 2 paws to the sides of the body at the shoulders.

## SPIKE BASE

With brown yarn, make a 6-st adjustable ring.

**Rnd 1:** Sc 2 in each sc around. (12 sts)

**Rnd 2:** *Sc 1, sc 2 in next sc; rep from * 5 more times. (18 sts)

**Rnd 3:** *Sc 2, sc 2 in next sc; rep from * 5 more times. (24 sts)

**Rnd 4:** *Sc 3, sc 2 in next sc; rep from * 5 more times. (30 sts)

**Rnds 5–13:** Sc 30.

**Rnd 14:** *Sc 3, sc2tog; rep from * 5 more times. (24 sts)

**Rnd 15:** Sc 24.

**Rnd 16:** *Sc 2, sc2tog; rep from * 5 more times. (18 sts)

**Rnds 17–20:** Sc 18.

**Rnd 21:** *Sc 1, sc2tog; rep from * 5 more times. (12 sts)

**Rnd 22:** Sc 12.

**Rnd 23:** *Sc 1, sc2tog; rep from * 3 more times. (8 sts)

Fasten off and weave yarn through remaining sts. Pull tightly to close hole.

Flatten the spike base and attach rnd 23 to top of the head and rnd 1 to the bottom of the body. Sew the edges of the spike base down to the back of the body.

For a not-too-spiky texture, apply a tight curl stitch to the surface of the spike base.

## TIGHT CURL STITCH

In surface sp or st, sl st 1, ch 1, sc 1 to rejoin yarn to surface of work, *ch 3, sk ch-3, sc 1 in ch-3 base st, sl st in next surface sp or st; rep from * until the spike base is covered **with** tight curls.

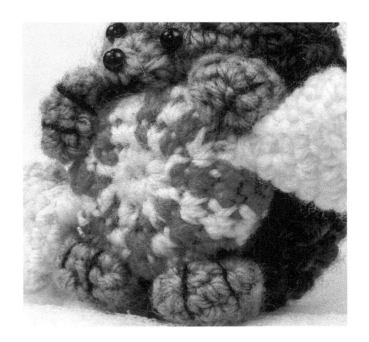

## PEPPERMINT

With white yarn, make an 8-st adjustable ring.

**Rnd 1:** (Sc 1 in white, sc 1 in red) in each st around. (16 sts)

**Rnd 2:** *Sc 2 in white in next st, sc 2 in red in next st; rep from * 7 more times. (32 sts)

**Rnds 3–4:** *Sc 2 in white, sc 2 in red; rep from * 7 more times. (32 sts)

**Rnd 5:** *Sc2tog in white, sc2tog in red; rep from * 7 more times. (16 sts)

**Cut red yarn. Cont in white.**

**Rnd 6:** Sc2tog 8 times. (8 sts)

**Rnd 7:** Sc 8.

Fasten off yarn, leaving a long tail for sewing.

Stuff peppermint. Weave yarn tail through remaining sts and pull to close hole. Flatten the peppermint slightly by drawing white yarn back and forth through the center of the mint to draw in and flatten the middle.

# HEDGEHOG (continued)

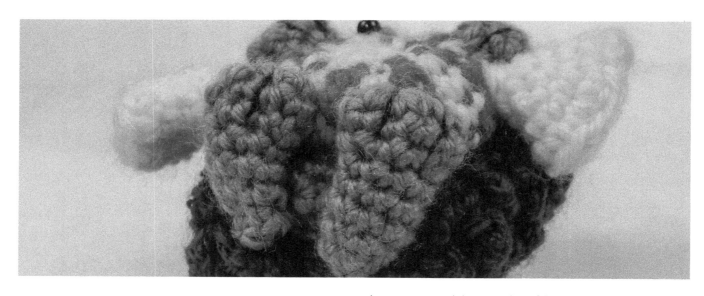

## WRAPPER (MAKE 2)

With white yarn, make a 6-st adjustable ring.

**Rnd 1:** Sc 6.

**Rnd 2:** *Sc 1, sc 2 in next st; rep from * 2 more times. (9 sts)

**Rnd 3:** *Sc 2, sc 2 in next st; rep from * 2 more times. (12 sts)

**Rnd 4:** *Sc 3, hdc 2 in next st; rep from * 2 more times. (15 sts)

Fasten off and weave in yarn tail.

Attach the smaller ends of the wrappers to sides of peppermint. Wrap the yarn tail around the point where the wrapper attaches to the peppermint 3 to 4 times. Fasten off and weave in end.

Attach completed peppermint to the front of the body. Wrap the arms around the top edge of the peppermint and secure in place with a few stitches. Apply a few stitches between the peppermint and the top of the feet to hold the pose in place. If needed, position the head so the chin overlaps the front of the peppermint and secure in place with a stitch or two.

With 3-strand black embroidery floss, embroider 2 long stitches over the front edges of each arm and foot for a paw detail.

Sew on a jump ring. Add a hanger (page 18).

# RABBIT

······ DIFFICULTY: INTERMEDIATE * FINISHED SIZE: 3" TALL, 2 1/2" WIDE (8 X 6 CM) ······

## ⇌ MATERIALS ⇌

- Sock weight yarn in green, ivory, red, and white
- Hook size C (2.75 mm)
- (2) 4 mm plastic eyes
- Craft glue
- Black embroidery floss
- Tapestry needle
- Pink acrylic paint
- Ear swab (cut in half on a slant)
- Scissors
- Metal comb or pet slicker brush
- Polyester fiberfill
- (1) 8–10 mm jump ring
- Place marker

## HEAD

With white yarn, ch 4.

**Rnd 1:** Starting in 2nd ch from hook and working in back ridge loops, sc 2, sc 5 in back ridge loop of next ch. Rotate ch so front loops are facing up. Starting in next ch and working in front loops, sc 1, sc 4 in fl of next ch. (12 sts)

**Rnd 2:** Sc 2 in next st, sc 1, sc 2 in next 5 sts, sc 1, sc 2 in next 4 sts. (22 sts)

**Rnd 3:** Sc 2, ch 2, sk ch-2, sk 2, sc 18. (22 sts)

**Rnd 4:** *Sc 7, sc2tog, sc 2; rep from * 1 more time. (20 sts)

**Rnd 5:** Sc 20.

**Rnd 6:** *Sc 2, sc2tog; rep from * 4 more times. (15 sts)

**Rnd 7:** Sc 15.

**Rnd 8:** *Sc 1, sc2tog; rep from * 4 more times. (10 sts)

**Rnd 9:** Sc 10.

Fasten off and stuff head. Close seam in a line with a mattress stitch at the bottom of the head.

## MUZZLE DETAIL

**Rnd 1:** Starting in lower right corner of muzzle opening, reattach white yarn (sl st 1, ch 1, sc 1) in same st (counts as first st). Cont to sc 7 more sts around the inside edge of the muzzle opening. (8 sts)

Fasten off in next st, leaving a long tail for sewing.

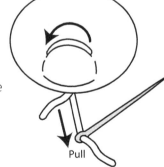

Pull

Thread yarn tail through the fl of rnd 1 and pull to close hole. Loop yarn over the front of the muzzle (from the middle of the muzzle to rnd 1 at the bottom of the head) 2 to 3 times, pulling firmly to cinch the lower half of the muzzle into two cheek shapes. Use leftover yarn tail to patch any holes in the sides of the muzzle.

Take (1) 12" (31 cm) length of white yarn and fasten it to the middle of rnd 1 at the bottom of the head. Draw the yarn up and out through the front of the head at rnd 4 slightly to

# RABBIT *(continued)*

the right of the muzzle. Reinsert needle slightly to the left of the muzzle at rnd 4 and draw out at the bottom of the head, pulling firmly to sink the bridge of the nose down into the head. Tie the yarn tails tog and weave knot and tails into the head.

Cover the stems of the plastic eyes with a bit of craft glue and insert above the muzzle with 3 sts of space between them.

Apply a small amount of pink acrylic paint to the cut end of the cotton swab. Gently tap the paint on to the nose area, allow to dry, and trim any loose yarn fibers that lifted during the painting process.

With 3-strand black embroidery floss, embroider a Y under the nose, a horizontal line for a mouth detail at the bottom of the Y, and a line over each eye for an eyebrow.

## EAR (MAKE 2)

With white yarn, ch 5.

**Rnd 1:** Starting in 2nd ch from hook and working in back ridge loops, sc 3, sc 5 in back ridge loop of next ch. Rotate ch so front loops are facing up. Starting in next ch and working in front loops, sc 3, ch 2. (11 sts)

Sl st to fasten off in next st, leaving a long tail for sewing.

Attach ears to top of head using the leftover yarn tail.

## BODY

With white yarn, make a 6-st adjustable ring.

**Rnd 1:** Sc 2 in each sc around. (12 sts)

**Rnd 2:** *Sc 2, sc 2 in next st; rep from * 3 more times. (16 sts)

**Rnd 3:** *Sc 3, sc 2 in next st; rep from * 3 more times. (20 sts)

**Rnd 4:** *Sc 4, sc 2 in next st; rep from * 3 more times. (24 sts)

**Rnd 5:** *Sc 4, sc2tog; rep from * 3 more times. (20 sts)

**Rnd 6:** Sc 20.

**Rnd 7:** *Sc 3, sc2tog; rep from * 3 more times. (16 sts)

**Rnds 8–9:** Sc 16.

**Rnd 10:** *Sc 2, sc2tog; rep from * 3 more times. (12 sts)

**Rnd 11:** Sc 12.

Stuff 50% full. Fasten off, leaving a long tail for sewing.

Flatten and sew rnd 11 of body closed. Sew to lower back of head (between rnds 2 and 3), allowing head to flop over the chest slightly. Sew bottom of chin to front of body to hold pose in place.

## PAW (MAKE 4)

With white yarn, ch 4.

**Rnd 1:** Starting in 2nd ch from hook and working in back ridge loops, sc 2, sc 4 in next ch. Rotate ch so front loops are facing up. Starting in next ch and working in front loops, sc 1, sc 3 in fl of next ch. (10 sts)

**Rnd 2:** Sc 10.

**Rnd 3:** Sc 3, sc2tog, sc 3, sc2tog. (8 sts)

**Rnds 4–5:** Sc 8.

**Rnd 6:** Sc 2, sc2tog, sc 2, sc2tog. (6 sts)

Lightly stuff.

**Rnd 7:** Sc 6.

Fasten off and weave yarn through remaining sts. Pull tightly to close hole.

For the feet, use leftover yarn tails to attach the top surface of 2 paws to bottom of the body with the larger ends facing up. For the hands, sew the smaller ends of the remaining 2 paws to the sides of the body at the shoulders.

## PEPPERMINT

With white yarn, make an 8-st adjustable ring.

**Rnd 1:** *(Sc 1 in white, sc 1 in red) in next st, (sc 1 in white, sc 1 in green) in next st; rep from * 3 more times. (16 sts)

**Rnd 2:** *Sc 2 in white in next st, sc 2 in red in next st, sc 2 in white in next st, sc 2 in green in next st; rep from * 3 more times. (32 sts)

# RABBIT *(continued)*

**Rnds 3–4:** *Sc 2 in white, sc 2 in red, sc 2 in white, sc 2 in green; rep from * 3 more times. (32 sts)

**Rnd 5:** *Sc2tog in white, sc2tog in red, sc2tog in white, sc-2tog in green; rep from * 3 more times. (16 sts)

**Cut red and green. Cont in white.**

**Rnd 6:** Sc2tog 8 times. (8 sts)

**Rnd 7:** Sc 8.

Fasten off, leaving a long tail for sewing.

Stuff peppermint. Weave yarn tail through remaining sts and pull to close hole. Flatten the peppermint slightly by drawing white yarn back and forth through the center of the mint to draw in and flatten the middle.

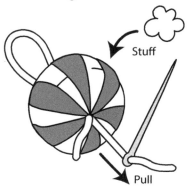

## WRAPPER (MAKE 2)

With white, make a 6-st adjustable ring.

**Rnd 1:** Sc 6.

**Rnd 2:** *Sc 1, sc 2 in next st; rep from * 2 more times. (9 sts)

**Rnd 3:** *Sc 2, sc 2 in next st; rep from * 2 more times. (12 sts)

**Rnd 4:** *Sc 3, hdc 2 in next st; rep from * 2 more times. (15 sts)

Fasten off and weave in yarn tail.

Attach the smaller ends of the wrappers to the sides of the peppermint. Wrap the yarn tail around the point where the wrapper attaches to the peppermint 3 to 4 times. Fasten off and weave in end.

Attach completed peppermint to the front of the body. Wrap the arms around the top edge of the peppermint and secure in place with a few stitches. Apply a few more stitches

between the peppermint and the top of the feet to hold the pose in place. If needed, position the head so the chin overlaps the front of the peppermint and secure in place with a stitch or two.

With 3-strand black embroidery floss, embroider 2 long stitches over the front edges of each arm and foot for a paw detail.

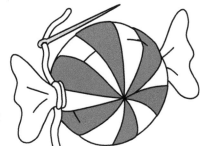

## TAIL

Wind ivory yarn around 4 fingers 30 times. Tie bundle tightly around the middle and cut the loops on both ends. Leave the yarn tails from the center of the bundle free and fluff the rest of the yarn by combing through the strands on either side. Trim so pom-pom measures about 1" (3 cm) across. Attach to back of rabbit with the yarn tails.

Sew on a jump ring. Add a hanger (page 18).

# SQUIRREL

······· DIFFICULTY: INTERMEDIATE * FINISHED SIZE: 2 1/2" TALL, 2 1/2" WIDE (6 X 6 CM) ·······

## ⇒ MATERIALS ⇐

- Sock weight yarn in gray, green, ivory, tan, and white
- Hook size C (2.75 mm)
- (2) 4 mm plastic eyes
- Craft glue
- Black embroidery floss
- Tapestry needle
- Scissors
- Polyester fiberfill
- Metal comb or pet slicker brush
- (1) 8–10 mm jump ring
- Place marker

## HEAD

With ivory yarn, ch 4.

**Rnd 1:** Starting in 2nd ch from hook and working in back ridge loops, sc 2, sc 5 in back ridge loop of next ch. Rotate ch so front loops are facing up. Starting in next ch and working in front loops, sc 1, sc 4 in fl of next ch. (12 sts)

**Rnd 2:** Sc 2 in next st, sc 1, sc 2 in next 5 sts, sc 1, sc 2 in next 4 sts. (22 sts)

**Cut ivory yarn. Change to gray.**

**Rnd 3:** Sc 2, ch 2, sk ch-2, sk 2, sc 18. (22 st)

**Rnd 4:** *Sc 7, sc2tog, sc 2; rep from * 1 more time. (20 sts)

**Rnd 5:** Sc 20.

**Rnd 6:** *Sc 2, sc2tog; rep from * 4 more times. (15 sts)

**Rnd 7:** Sc 15.

**Rnd 8:** *Sc 1, sc2tog; rep from * 4 more times. (10 sts)

**Rnd 9:** Sc 10.

Fasten off and stuff head. Close seam in a line with a mattress stitch at the bottom of the head.

## MUZZLE DETAIL

Start with ivory yarn.

**Rnd 1:** Starting in lower right corner of muzzle opening, reattach yarn (sl st 1, ch 1, sc 1) in same st (counts as first st). Cont to sc 7 more sts around the inside edge of the muzzle opening. (8 sts)

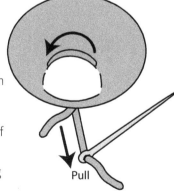

Pull

Fasten off in next st, leaving a long tail for sewing.

Thread yarn tail through the fl of rnd 1 and pull to close hole. Loop yarn over the front of the muzzle (from the middle of the muzzle to rnd 1 at the bottom of the head) 2 to 3 times, pulling firmly to cinch the lower half of the muzzle into two cheek shapes. Use leftover yarn tail to patch any holes in the sides of the muzzle.

# SQUIRREL *(continued)*

Take (1) 12" (31 cm) length of gray yarn and fasten it to the middle of rnd 1 at the bottom of the head. Draw the yarn up and out of the front of the head at rnd 4 slightly to the right of the muzzle. Reinsert needle slightly to the left of the muzzle and draw out at the bottom of the head, pulling firmly to sink the bridge of the nose down. Tie the yarn tails tog and weave knot and tails into the head.

Cover the stems of the plastic eyes with a bit of craft glue and insert above the muzzle with 3 sts of space between them.

With 3-strand black embroidery floss, embroider an Y onto the front of the muzzle for a nose, a horizontal line at the bottom of the Y for a mouth detail, and a line over each eye for an eyebrow. With tan yarn, apply 3 to 4 closely packed vertical satin stitches within the V shape at the top of the Y.

## EAR (MAKE 2)

With gray yarn, make a 4-st adjustable ring, ch 1, turn.

**Row 1:** Sk ch 1, sl st 1, sc 1, ch 2, sc 1, sl st 1.

Fasten off, leaving a long tail for sewing.

Sew first and last st of row 1 tog to pinch base of ear tog. Sew ears to upper half of head.

Cut (2) 4" (10 cm) pieces of gray yarn and attach to ch-2 sp at the top of the ears with a fringe knot. Separate yarn plies, brush through with a comb to fluff, and trim to shape.

## BODY

With gray yarn, make a 6-st adjustable ring.

**Rnd 1:** Sc 2 in each sc around. (12 sts)

**Rnd 2:** *Sc 2, sc 2 in next st; rep from * 3 more times. (16 sts)

**Rnd 3:** *Sc 3, sc 2 in next st; rep from * 3 more times. (20 sts)

**Rnd 4:** *Sc 4, sc 2 in next st; rep from * 3 more times. (24 sts)

**Rnd 5:** *Sc 4, sc2tog; rep from * 3 more times. (20 sts)

**Rnd 6:** Sc 20.

**Rnd 7:** *Sc 3, sc2tog; rep from * 3 more times. (16 sts)

**Rnds 8–9:** Sc 16.

**Rnd 10:** *Sc 2, sc2tog; rep from * 3 more times. (12 sts)

**Rnd 11:** Sc 12.

Stuff 50%. Fasten off, leaving a long tail for sewing.

Flatten and sew rnd 11 of body closed. Sew to lower back of head (between rnds 2–3), allowing head to flop over the chest slightly. Sew bottom of chin to front of body to hold pose in place.

# SQUIRREL *(continued)*

## TAIL

With gray yarn, make a 6-st adjustable ring.

**Rnd 1:** Sc 2 in each sc around. (12 sts)

**Rnd 2:** *Sc 2, sc 2 in next st; rep from * 3 more times. (16 sts)

**Rnd 3:** *Sc 3 sc 2 in next st; rep from * 3 more times. (20 sts)

**Rnd 4:** *Sc 4, sc 2 in next st; rep from * 3 more times. (24 sts)

**Rnds 5–6:** Sc 24.

**Rnd 7:** *Sc 4, sc2tog; rep from * 3 more times. (20 sts)

**Rnds 8–13:** Sc 20.

**Rnd 14:** *Sc 3, sc2tog; rep from * 3 more times. (16 sts)

**Rnds 15–17:** Sc 16.

**Rnd 18:** *Sc 2, sc2tog; rep from * 3 more times. (12 sts)

**Rnd 19:** Sc 12.

Stuff 50% full. Fasten off, leaving a long tail for sewing.

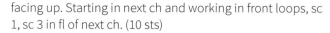

With metal comb or a pet slicker brush, brush surface of tail to lift yarn fibers until stitches are fairly obscured by fuzz. Sew rnd 1 to bottom back side of body and secure inside surface of tail to back surface of body (leaving the last 8 rnds of the tail free). Curl over top of tail and secure by sewing rnd 19 down to the back surface of the tail with a few stitches.

## PAW (MAKE 4)

With ivory, ch 4.

**Rnd 1:** Starting in 2nd ch from hook and working in back ridge loops, sc 2, sc 4 in next ch. Rotate ch so front loops are facing up. Starting in next ch and working in front loops, sc 1, sc 3 in fl of next ch. (10 sts)

**Rnd 2:** Sc 10.

**Cut ivory yarn. Change to gray.**

**Rnd 3:** *Sc 3, sc2tog; rep from * 1 more time. (8 sts)

**Rnds 4–5:** Sc 8.

**Rnd 6:** *Sc 2, sc2tog; rep from * 1 more time. (6 sts)

**Lightly stuff.**

**Rnd 7:** Sc 6.

Fasten off and weave yarn through remaining sts. Pull tightly to close hole.

For the feet, use leftover yarn tails to attach the top surface of two paws to bottom of the body with the larger ends facing up. For the hands, sew the smaller ends of the remaining 2 paws to the sides of the body at the shoulders.

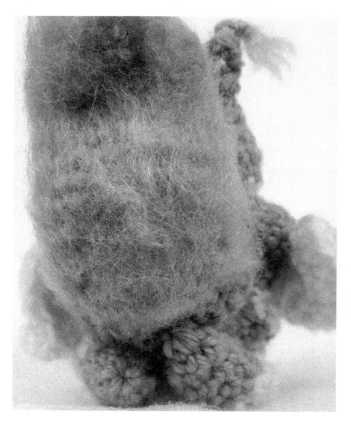

## PEPPERMINT

With white yarn, make an 8-st adjustable ring.

**Rnd 1:** (Sc 1 in white, sc 1 in green) in each st around. (16 sts)

**Rnd 2:** *(Sc 2 in white) in next st, (sc 2 in green) in next st; rep from * 7 more times. (32 sts)

**Rnds 3–4:** *Sc 2 in white, sc 2 in green; rep from * 7 more times. (32 sts)

**Rnd 5:** *Sc2tog in white, sc2tog in green; rep from * 7 more times. (16 sts)

**Cut green yarn. Cont in white.**

**Rnd 6:** Sc2tog 8 times. (8 sts)

**Rnd 7:** Sc 8.

Fasten off, leaving a long tail for sewing.

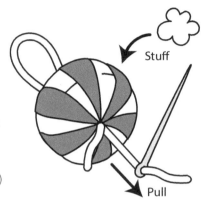

Stuff peppermint. Weave yarn tail through remaining sts and pull to close hole. Flatten the peppermint slightly by drawing white yarn back and forth through the center of the mint to draw in and flatten the middle.

## WRAPPER (MAKE 2)

With white yarn, make a 6-st adjustable ring.

**Rnd 1:** Sc 6.

**Rnd 2:** *Sc 1, sc 2 in next st; rep from * 2 more times. (9 sts)

**Rnd 3:** *Sc 2, sc 2 in next st; rep from * 2 more times. (12 sts)

**Rnd 4:** *Sc 3, hdc 2 in next st; rep from * 2 more times.

(15 sts)

Fasten off and weave in yarn tail.

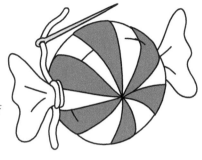

Attach the smaller ends of the wrappers to the sides of **the** peppermint. Wrap the yarn tail around the point where the wrapper attaches to the peppermint 3 to 4 times. Fasten off and weave in end.

Attach completed peppermint to the front of the body. Wrap the arms around the top edge of the peppermint and secure in place with a few stitches. Apply a few stitches between the peppermint and the top of the feet to hold the pose in place. If needed, position the head so the chin overlaps the front of the peppermint and secure in place with a stitch or two.

With 3-strand black embroidery floss, embroider 2 long stitches over the front edges of each arm and foot for a paw detail.

Sew on a jump ring. Add a hanger (page 18).

# RESOURCES

## ABBREVIATIONS

\* Repeat instructions following the asterisk[s] as directed

| | |
|---|---|
| approx | approximately |
| beg | begin(ning) |
| bl | back loop(s) |
| BPsc | back post single crochet |
| CC | contrasting color |
| ch(s) | chain(s) or chain stitch(es) |
| ch- | refers to chain, or chain space previously made, such as "ch-1 space" |
| cont | continue(ing)(s) |
| dc | double crochet(s) |
| dec(s) | decrease(ing)(s) |
| fl | front loop(s) |
| FPsc | front post single crochet |
| hdc | half double crochet(s) |
| hdc2tog | half double crochet 2 stitches together—1 stitch decreased |
| inc(s) | increase(ing)(s) |
| lp(s) | loop(s) |
| MC | main color |
| mm | millimeter |
| pm | place marker |
| rep(s) | repeat(s) |
| rnd(s) | round(s) |
| RS | right side |
| sc | single crochet(s) |
| sc2tog | single crochet 2 stitches together—1 stitch decreased |
| sk | skip |
| sl | slip |
| sl st(s) | slip stitch(es) |
| sp(s) | space(s) |
| st(s) | stitch(es) |
| tog | together |
| tr | treble crochet |
| WS | wrong side |
| YO(s) | yarn over(s) |
| yd(s) | yard(s) |

## PROJECT RANKING

**Beginner:** Projects for first-time crocheters using basic stitches; minimal shaping.

**Easy:** Projects using yarn with basic stitches, repetitive stitch patterns, simple color changes, and simple shaping and finishing.

**Intermediate:** Projects using a variety of techniques, such as basic lace patterns or color patterns; midlevel shaping and finishing.

**Experienced:** Projects with intricate stitch patterns, techniques, and dimension, such as non-repeating patterns, multicolor techniques, fine threads, small hooks, detailed shaping, and refined finishing.

## CROCHET HOOK SIZES

| Millimeter | U.S. Size* |
|---|---|
| 2.25 mm | B-1 |
| 2.75 mm | C-2 |
| 3.25 mm | D-3 |
| 3.5 mm | E-4 |
| 3.75 mm | F-5 |
| 4 mm | G-6 |
| 4.5 mm | 7 |
| 5 mm | H-8 |
| 5.5 mm | I-9 |
| 6 mm | J-10 |
| 6.5 mm | K-10½ |
| 8 mm | L-11 |
| 9 mm | M/N-13 |

*Letter or number may vary. Rely on the millimeter sizing.

# YARN WEIGHT CHART

| Yarn Weight Symbol & Category Names | ( 0 ) LACE | ( 1 ) SUPER FINE | ( 2 ) FINE | ( 3 ) LIGHT | ( 4 ) MEDIUM | ( 5 ) BULKY | ( 6 ) SUPER BULKY | ( 7 ) JUMBO |
|---|---|---|---|---|---|---|---|---|
| Types of Yarns in Category | Fingering, 10 count crochet thread | Sock, Fingering, Baby | Sport, Baby | DK, Light Worsted | Worsted, Afghan, Aran | Chunky, Craft, Rug | Bulky, Roving | Jumbo, Roving |

Source: Craft Yarn Council's www.YarnStandards.com

## MATERIAL SOURCES

If you're interested in using some of the yarns or tools used in this book, please check out the following resources!

**6060**
www.6060.etsy.com
Online retailer of a unique variety of plastic safety eyes

**American Felt & Craft**
www.americanfeltandcraft.com
Online retailer of fine wool felts

**Cascade Yarn**
www.cascadeyarn.com
Wholesaler and distributor of fine yarns

**Clover**
www.clover-usa.com
Hooks and notions, available at local craft stores

**Delta Sobo Craft Glue**
www.plaidonline.com
Glue and craft supplies

**Fiskars**
www.fiskars.com
Scissors and cutting mats, available at local craft stores

**Glass Eyes Online**
www.glasseyesonline.com
An international source of glass and safety eyes

**Hobbs Bonded Fibers**
www.hobbsbondedfibers.com
Poly-down fiberfill toy stuffing and black batting, available at local craft stores

## METRIC CONVERSIONS

In this book, I've mostly used inch measurements, with anything less than one shown as a fraction.

If you want to convert those to metric measurements, please use the following formulas:

**Fractions to Decimals**

$1/8 = .125$

$1/4 = .25$

$1/2 = .5$

$5/8 = .625$

$3/4 = .75$

**Imperial to Metric Conversion**

Multiply inches by 25.4 to get millimeters

Multiply inches by 2.54 to get centimeters

For example, if you wanted to convert $1\frac{1}{8}$ inches to millimeters:

1.125 in. x 25.4 mm = 28.575 mm

## PROJECT COLORS

All of the projects in this book were made using Cascade Heritage 150 sock weight yarn in the colors outlined below. Feel free to use your favorite brand of sock weight yarn (available online and through your local yarn shop).

### 12 Days of Christmas

Partridge in a Pear Tree: red (5607), bark (5609), camel (5610), snow (5618), jade (5627), blood orange (5642), real black (5672), gold fusion (5723), frost gray (5755)

Turtle Doves: snow (5618), charcoal (5631), real black (5672), frost gray (5755), orchid (5757)

French Hen: red (5607), camel (5610), fuschia (5616), Italian plum (5633), real black (5672), China blue (5686), grape juice (5706), gold fusion (5723), Caribbean Sea (5753)

Calling Bird: snow (5618), charcoal (5631), lemon (5644), China blue (5686)

Golden Rings: gold fusion (5723)

Goose a-Laying: camel (5610), charcoal (5631), cinnamon (5640), real black (5672),white (5682), gold fusion (5723), frost gray (5755)

Swan a-Swimming: cinnamon (5640), real black (5672), white (5682)

Maid a-Milking: denim (5604), bark (5609), camel (5610), lemon (5644), white (5682), frost gray (5755)

Lady Dancing: bark (5609), camel (5610), fuschia (5616), snow (5618), white (5682), Caribbean Sea (5753)

Lord a-Leaping: plum (5605), bark (5609), camel (5610), lilac (5614), real black (5672), white (5682)

Piper Piping: bark (5609), camel (5610), snow (5618), navy (5623), real black (5672), white (5682), gold fusion (5723)

Drummer Drumming: red (5607), camel (5610), real black (5672), white (5682), gold fusion (5723), Caribbean Sea (5753), frost gray (5755)

### Winter Flora

Pinecone: bark (5609)

Holly: red (5607), pine (5608)

Mistletoe: jade (5627)

Poinsettia: red (5607), jade (5627)

Pickle: moss (5612)

### The Nutcracker

Sugar Plum Fairy: camel (5610), moss (5612), lilac (5614), white (5682), grape juice (5706), orchid (5757)

Nutcracker: red (5607), camel (5610), snow (5618), real black (5672), white (5682), gold fusion (5723)

Clara: bark (5609), camel (5610), fuschia (5616), lemon (5644), white (5682)

Mouse King: tutu (5613), snow (5618), real black (5672), white (5682), gold fusion (5723), frost gray (5755)

### Gifts from Santa

Train Engine: red (5607), pine (5608), real black (5672), white (5682), gold fusion (5723), frost gray (5755)

Puppy in Square Box: real black (5672), white (5682), deep ocean (5720), frost gray (5755)

Kitty in Round Box: camel (5610), tutu (5613), fuschia (5616), white (5682)

Rocking Horse: camel (5610), brown (5639), real black (5672)

Rag Doll: camel (5610), zinnia red (5661), white (5682), Caribbean Sea (5753)

Socks: red (5607), Christmas green (5656)

Lump of Coal: real black (5672)

### Deck the Halls

Tree Lights: red (5607), pine (5608), turquoise (5626), white (5682), gold fusion (5723)

Ringing Bell: moss (5612), lemon (5644)

Sleigh Bell: real black (5672), white (5682), China blue (5686)

Wreath: pine (5608), moss (5612), brown (5639), grape juice (5706)

Candle: mango (5641), lemon (5644), zinnia red (5661), real black (5672), white (5682), gold fusion (5723)

### Peppermint Pals

Hedgehog: red (5607), camel (5610), brown (5639), white (5682)

Rabbit: red (5607), snow (5618), Christmas green (5656), white (5682)

Squirrel: camel (5610), snow (5618), Christmas green (5656), white (5682), frost gray (5755)

# ABOUT THE AUTHOR

Megan Kreiner grew up on Long Island, New York, in a household where arts and crafts were a part of daily life. She learned how to knit at an early age from her grandmother, aunt, and mother, and began designing toy patterns for her son soon after teaching herself how to crochet. Since 2012, her MK Crochet & Knits patterns have been published and featured in numerous crochet and knitting magazines, kits, and books.

Outside of her work in stitchcraft, Megan's professional credits include over fifteen animated feature films as well as short films, television shows, and theme-park attractions for world-renowned studios such as Sony Pictures Imageworks, DreamWorks Animation, and Walt Disney Animation Studios.

Megan lives in Los Angeles, California with her husband, Michael; children, James and Emily; and cat, Olive. View her work at www.mkcrochetandknits.com.

*mk crochet* ®

## ACKNOWLEDGMENTS

Thank you to my agent, Amanda Luedeke, for keeping me on track, for encouraging me when life gets complicated, and for being genuinely supportive of all my crazy concepts. You are the voice of reason and I am very grateful!

Thank you to my publisher, Paul McGahren, at Cedar Lane Press for supporting another round of holiday-themed craziness by allowing me an opportunity to publish this second collection of ornaments!

Thank you to Cascade Yarns for their generous contribution of yarn for this book.

And, as always, thank you to my husband, Michael, who turns a blind eye to the flurry of yarn that takes over our living room during the pattern-writing process and to my children, James and Emily, for providing me with their tough but fair brand of project critiques. Your support is the gift that keeps on giving!

# INDEX

*Italicized text indicates a project

abbreviations, 144
*Calling Bird, 33*
*Candle, 126*
*Christmas Pickle, 74*
*Clara, 86*
crochet hook sizes, 144
crochet stitches
    back post single crochet, 12
    chain, 11
    decreases, 13
    double crochet, 12
    double crochet decrease, 13
    front post single crochet, 12
    half double crochet, 11
    half-double crochet decrease, 13
    increases, 13
    invisible single-crochet decrease, 13
    single crochet, 11
    single crochet 3 together, 13
    single crochet 4 together, 13
    single-crochet decrease, 13
    skip, 13
    slip stitch, 11
    slipknot, 11
    treble crochet, 12
    working in back loops, 13
    working in both loops, 13
    working in front loops, 13
    yarn over, 11
crochet techniques
    adjustable ring, 14

changing colors, 14
covering a cabone ring, 15
right side, 14
surface loops, 15
twisted cords, 15
working around a chain, 14
working in a chain space, 14
working in rows, 14
working in surface stitches, 15
working in the round, 14
wrong side, 14
*Drummer Drumming, 60*
finishing stitches
    chain stitch, 17
    closing round holes, 16
    couching, 17
    fringe knots, 17
    lazy daisy, 17
    long stitch, 16
    mattress stitch, 16
    overcast stitch, 17
    running stitch, 16
    satin stitch, 16
    whip stitch, 16
*French Hen, 30*
*Golden Rings, 36*
*Goose a-Laying, 38*
hangers
    customizing, 19
    making, 18
    templates, 19
*Hedgehog, 130*

*Holly, 68*
jump ring, attaching, 18
*Kitty in Round Gift Box, 103*
*Lady Dancing, 48*
*Lord a-Leaping, 52*
*Lump of Coal, 117*
*Maid a-Milking, 44*
material sources, 145
metric conversions, 145
*Mistletoe, 70*
*Mouse King, 89*
*Nutcracker, 81*
*Partridge in a Pear Tree, 22*
*Pinecone, 66*
*Piper Piping, 56*
*Poinsettia, 72*
project colors, 146
*Puppy in Square Gift Box, 99*
*Rabbit, 135*
*Rag Doll, 113*
*Ringing Bell, 122*
*Rocking Horse, 108*
*Sleigh Bell, 123*
*Socks, 116*
*Squirrel, 139*
*Sugarplum Fairy, 78*
*Swan a-Swimming, 41*
template
    crook hanger, 19
    hangers, 19
    headpin hanger, 19
    headpin, 19
    simple hangers, 19

"S" hanger, 19
"U" hanger, 19
*Train Engine, 94*
*Tree Lights, 120*
tools and materials
    beads, 9
    crochet hooks, 8
    felt, 8
    glitter, 10
    glue, 9
    jump rings, 9
    marking pins, 10
    metallic paint pen, 19
    needles, 8
    paint, puff, 10
    plastic eyes, 9
    project bags, 10
    ribbons, 10
    scissors, 8
    split or locking rings, 10
    stickers, 19
    stitch counter, 10
    stuffing, 8
    tackle box, 10
    thread, 9
    twine, 10
    wire, 10
    wire tools, 10
    yarn, 8
    wire bending tips, 18
*Turtle Doves, 26*
*Wreath, 124*
yarn weights, 145

## PROJECT INDEX BY DIFFICULTY

**Beginner**
Lump of Coal, 117

**Easy**
Christmas Pickle, 74
Golden Rings, 36
Holly, 68
Mistletoe, 70
Pinecone, 66
Poinsettia, 72
Ringing Bell, 122
Sleigh Bell, 123
Socks, 116
Tree Lights, 120

**Intermediate**
Calling Bird, 33
Candle, 126
Clara, 86
Drummer Drumming, 60
French Hen, 30
Goose a-Laying, 38
Hedgehog, 130
Kitty In Round Gift Box, 103
Lady Dancing, 48
Lord a-Leaping, 52
Maid a-Milking, 44
Mouse King, 89

Nutcracker, 81
Partridge in a Pear Tree, 22
Piper Piping, 56
Puppy in Square Gift Box, 99
Rabbit, 135
Rag Doll, 113
Rocking Horse, 108
Squirrel, 139
Sugarplum Fairy, 78
Swan a-Swimming, 41
Train Engine, 94
Turtle Doves, 26
Wreath, 124

### Christmas Ornaments to Crochet
#### 31 Festive & Fun Designs for a Handmade Holiday
$24.95 | 128 Pages

When you crochet any of the 31 projects in *Christmas Ornaments to Crochet*, you're spending a few creative hours to craft a gift that will be cherished for years. Each design will appeal to the beginner and advanced crafter alike and they can stand alone or be part of a complete set, like a nativity scene or Santa at the North Pole. Helpful techniques ensure success and tips for adding a personal touch are provided. The ornaments in *Christmas Ornaments to Crochet* will be a prized addition to any Christmas tree this holiday season.

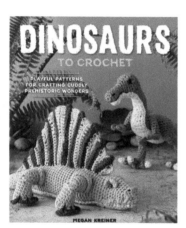

### Dinosaurs to Crochet
#### Playful Patterns for Crafting Cuddly Prehistoric Wonders
$24.95 | 126 Pages

Old-fashioned playtime will never go extinct with this collection of huggable dinosaurs and their friendly reptilian sidekicks, all made from quick-to-hook chunky yarn. With a few basic stitches and the imaginative designs of best-selling author Megan Kreiner, crafters can create a fearsomely fun tyrannosaurus, a cuddly stegosaurus, a flying pteranodon, or a spiky ankylosaurus. The extensive how-to section featuring step-by-step stitches, construction techniques, and finishing tips guarantees success. More than a crochet book, *Dinosaurs to Crochet* delivers hours of imaginative playtime for even the most discerning paleontologist in training.

### Construction Vehicles to Crochet
#### Chunky Trucks & Marvelous Machines Straight from the Building Site
$24.95 | 120 Pages

Get ready to crochet an entire construction site of chunky trucks and marvelous machines! Whether your little one loves bulldozers, cranes, cement mixers, or dump trucks, you'll find a machine to please. And, with moving parts, each construction vehicle will provide hours of make-believe scooping, plowing, and steamrolling fun. Additional projects like safety cones, rocks, and crates will add to the buzzing scene of a building site. Packed with step-by-step instructions, helpful illustrations, and full-color photography, *Construction Vehicles to Crochet* will have your favorite construction fan playing at the building site all day long.

CEDAR LANE PRESS

Look for this title wherever books are sold or visit www.cedarlanepress.com.

Printed in the USA
CPSIA information can be obtained
at www.ICGtesting.com
JSHW040914290824
68930JS00006B/7

9 781958 212120